Poor Man's Philanthropist

The Thomas Cannon Story

Thomas and Princetta Cannon, 1963 (Family Photo)

By Sandra Waugaman

with Thomas Cannon

Poor Man's Philanthropist

The Thomas Cannon Story

*TO SOHILA,
I REALLY APPRECIATE YOUR
ESSAY ABOUT MY DAD,
THE FUTURE IS YOURS.*

By Sandra Waugaman

with Thomas Cannon

*Thomas Cannon, Jr
2/3/16*

palari
Publishing

Richmond, VA

Poor Man's Philanthropist:

The Thomas Cannon Story

© 2004, By Sandra Waugaman, Thomas Cannon

Published by Palari Publishing

www.palaribooks.com

Permissions Department

Palari Publishing

PO Box 9288

Richmond, VA 23227-0288

Library of Congress Cataloging-in-Publication Data
Waugaman, Sandra F.
    The poor man's philanthropist : the Thomas Cannon story / by Sandra Waugaman ; with Thomas Cannon.
        p. cm.
    Includes index.
    ISBN 1-928662-05-6 (hardcover)
    1. Cannon, Thomas, 1925- 2. Philanthropists--Virginia--Biography. I. Cannon, Thomas, 1925- II. Title.
    HV28.C24W38 2004
    361.7'4'092--dc22

2004013296

ISBN: 1-928662-05-6

Printed in the United States of America

For Craig, an inspiration to all who knew him.

Acknowledgements

All books begin with an idea, one that has usually been growing and taking shape in the writer's mind for months or even years. That's not the case with this book. It was not this writer's idea. David Smitherman of Palari Publishing asked me what I thought about doing a book on Thomas Cannon, and I thought he had a wonderful idea. On reflection, I wondered why no one had thought of it sooner. I am extremely grateful to him for giving me the opportunity to write this book and to get to know such a remarkable person.

I am also thankful that Thomas Cannon agreed to the idea and was willing to let me write his story. It was to be a story about his philanthropy, and he kept excellent records about his gifts and the people whose lives he had touched. He shared clippings, stories and photos with me that he had carefully filed in large brown envelopes numbered according to the order in which he presented his checks. But his story became more than one about his compassion and generosity. It touches upon some major historic times in our country because of his experiences with segregation, World War II and prejudice. It also shows how one man can overcome poverty, personal disappointments and anger, and grow to become an inspiration to others.

There are too many people who graciously shared their stories with me to be listed here — and they are mentioned in the book — but I do thank them for their cooperation.

On a more personal note, I have to acknowledge my husband, Si, who gave up both dinner and the use of the telephone many nights, and my son, Chris, who had to listen to constant updates on the book and do a good bit of proofreading.
—Sandra Waugaman

Acknowledgements

Thanks:

To Sandy — for writing my story.

To David — for publishing my story.

To Gary — for being the greatest benefactor I've ever had.

To Jenny — for being the lovingest, most supportive daughter-in-law a man could have.

To T.C. — for marrying Jenny.

To Rachel — for a lifetime of sisterly love and support.

To Jill — for being our "legal eagle" and a loving, supportive family friend.

To Maggie — for warm, supportive friendship and for turning me into a "theater critic."

To Katie — for loving, supportive friendship and for standing up to critics who "put me down."

To Joe — for being my best buddy and "cheerleader."

To all friends, relatives and supporters not listed above — thanks, thanks and thanks again

—Thomas Cannon

Table of Contents

Chapter 1

Cannon's Gift

July 22, 2003

Dear Mr. Lohmann,

You have kindly and graciously served as my intermediary in the past, so I come to you again to seek your help.

This morning I read your article in the Richmond Times-Dispatch about Ms. Tina Johnson ("Cancer battle painful in more ways than one").

The expression "when it rains it pours" surely describes the soul-shattering ordeal of Tina Johnson. It seems as if the forces of Fate itself have conspired to make this poor woman's life a living nightmare.

The financial needs of Ms. Johnson and her family are far beyond my ability to really make any meaningful difference in their lives. Nevertheless, I wish to donate the enclosed $1,000 check to her to let her see that I and others (like YOU) care about her, her daughters and her nieces.

At least this check will help Ms. Johnson with some of the basic necessities until she is back on the job.

Tina Johnson is an incredibly strong and courageous woman. I respect and admire her very much for her strength, her faith and her perseverance against overwhelming obstacles in her life. I regret not being in a position to render much more assistance to such a brave and deserving mother and aunt.

Please pass my check to Ms. Tina Johnson — along with the poems and the "Hug" coupon. I thank you very much for your interest in her story and for bringing that story to my attention and thereby making this gift to her possible.

Very cordially yours,
Tom Cannon

When Tina Johnson walked across her dining room, water oozed up through the carpet and squished between her toes. She knew something was wrong. Although the water wasn't immediately visible, it had been seeping through the walls and into her two-bedroom condominium for quite some time.

The summer of 2003 had been unusually rainy for Richmond, Virginia. There had been instances of street flooding, and warnings of severe thunderstorms and flash flooding had been creeping across the screens of TV viewers for months. Tina didn't know it, but the walls of her ground-floor apartment had not been waterproofed properly when the condo was constructed, which was why water was seeping through them.

The sogginess of her home was just the latest in a series of problems that only seemed to get worse as the days passed for Tina and her family.

When her sister died from breast cancer in 1999, she left behind three teenage girls. Each girl had a different father. One was incarcerated so he couldn't take care of his daughter, another thought the girl would be better off if she lived with Tina, and the third took Tina to court to get custody of his daughter. But the girls wanted to stay together, and they all wanted to live with their Aunt Tina. So she fought the court case and eventually was awarded custody of all three girls. They settled into the modest two-bedroom condominium with Tina, and her own twin teenage girls.

A month later, Tina's husband decided to move out. She found herself on her own with five teenage girls to raise. Although they were cramped and crowded and the girls had to share beds, they were getting by while she was working as an insurance analyst. But when the unthinkable happened, and her 15-year-old niece Jessica developed breast cancer, Tina had to take a leave of absence from her job.

Tina was paid during her time off, but the Federal Family and Medical Leave Act allows for only 12 weeks. When that time expired, her employer had to let her go. Without a job, and still taking care of Jessica after her surgery and chemotherapy treatments, it seemed things couldn't get much worse. But they did. She found that not only had water seeped into the apartment, but when they pulled the beds away from the walls and moved the boxes of shoes that were stacked against one wall and stored under the bed, they found mold growing every-where. Up the walls, on the mattresses, and on their shoes. They had to get rid of the moldy things, and they all crowded together into the one room not affected by the mold or water – the living room. Four of them slept on the floor and one girl slept on the sofa.

Tina says, "I asked if we could be provided a place to stay while they corrected the problem since it was a construction issue. But while the owners agreed it was a problem they would have to fix, they said that it wasn't possible to move us. So we had no place to go and had to stay in the apartment while work went on.

"They sent mold technicians in to try to correct the problem, but as they began to work on the walls I guess the mold became a little more airborne and about two weeks after they started checking it, I started coughing in my sleep. It got so bad that I actually couldn't breathe, and I would wake up coughing and even vomiting. That's when the doctor put me on a nebulizer nightly because he said I was having an allergic reaction to the mold. I was starting to get a little nervous because at first my breathing was only bothering me at night, but then it started to bother me during the day. It got to where I couldn't go for a walk with my daughter. I couldn't catch my breath. My chest got to the point that I was getting sharp pains every time I tried to inhale. Exhaling did not hurt, but just trying to inhale a soft breath would give me a pain in my chest."

Tina applied for emergency help, but was told that she made too much money to qualify because of her unemployment payments.

After trying all the agencies she could think of, she was steered to the Legal Information Network for Cancer, (LINC) a nonprofit, community-based volunteer organization that helps people with the nonmedical side of cancer.

She went to LINC and they took down her information. Shortly after her papers were placed on the director's desk, a phone call came in from Bill Lohmann.

Bill was trying to tie one of his columns on family life in Richmond in with a comic strip that had been running in the local newspaper about a young woman with cancer who found a lawyer through an agency like LINC. When he called the Richmond group, Tina Johnson's papers were sitting on the desk, and Bill had his column.

After reading Tina Johnson's story in the newspaper, Thomas Cannon decided to try to help her and her family. He sent a $1,000 check, some inspirational poems, a coupon for a hug, and a letter to Bill who then called Tina. When Bill gave her the envelope with the check in it, he explained that Mr. Cannon was a retired postal worker who saved his money and lived very modestly so that he could make gifts like this periodically. He says, "She was opening the envelope as I was talking, and when she saw that the check was for $1,000, she was completely stunned. She put her hands over her face and couldn't say anything for a few minutes. I've delivered more than half a dozen checks for Mr. Cannon, and people usually have that reaction. They can't believe the check is for them. One man even broke into tears, but usually people just don't know what to say. Mr. Cannon has the knack of picking very humble people who don't realize they are doing anything special, and so they are surprised when someone does something like that for them."

Tina says, "Maybe $1,000 isn't a lot of money to

some people, but when you're financially tapped out because of medical bills and other problems, that can be a very, very large sum. I was completely blown away, because not only was this a large check but this check was from someone who didn't know me. The letter to Bill Lohmann was also in the envelope and it had Mr. Cannon's phone number on it, so I had to call and tell him how grateful my daughters and I were for his monetary gift."

The check enabled Tina to buy five beds. She bought each girl a futon so they didn't have to sleep on the floor anymore. Other smaller donations had also come in after the article appeared in the newspaper, so she was able to pay off past bills, including ones that had mounted up after Jessica's medical treatments. By then they had also found a new apartment, and were getting ready to move. But when Tina thought about Tom's gift, she says, "The money was nice, but it was the heart behind it that was the important thing. The fact that he made the gift with a loving heart, and he did it for someone he didn't know. That was a tremendous blessing because it gave me the opportunity to show my girls that there are people out there who are willing to help others, and not look for anything back. It was a life lesson for them. He was not looking for any praise, he just wanted to help relieve the stress of another person. I'm not a family member of his, I'm not a friend of the family, or even a friend of a friend – I'm a complete stranger that he did not know, but God put it on his heart to help me and bless me, and he did it with a willing heart."

Tina is also a giving person. Although she never has money to give to people, she gives of her time and love. It was getting to the point that her girls were starting to resent the fact that she did so much for others because when she needed help nobody seemed to care. She says, "We were talking, and I asked them why they got upset about me doing things for other people, and one of my daughters replied that I was always doing for everyone else, but nobody did anything for us." That's when Tom's gift arrived and changed their outlook.

His checks often arrive at just the right time to give someone a spiritual lift or helping hand. Bill says he remembers hearing about Thomas Cannon when he was growing up in Richmond, and so he's honored when he is asked to deliver one of the checks.

Chapter 2

Chase City, Virginia

Thomas Cannon (Family Photo)

As the train left Richmond and rumbled through Central Virginia heading south, the houses became further apart and forests, fields, and neatly planted rows of crops more frequent. Soon the train was in tobacco country, and the train whistle signaled its approach to the stop at Chase City.

Newly widowed Eliza Cannon got off the train there with her four children – Ben, Joe, Ruth and Thomas. She had come home to live with her mother, Luna and stepfather, William Haskins because she had no place else to go.

In 1928 it was hard enough for most families to survive, but for a woman whose husband had died without insurance, leaving her penniless, things looked very bleak. She didn't even have enough money to bury him, but the owner of a funeral home understood her situation and graciously offered to absorb the costs. She and her children left Richmond with little more than the clothes on their backs and the hope that her family would take them in.

It's difficult for a three-year-old to remember much about his father, but Thomas has a vague memory of him being laid out in the living room of their home in Richmond, and people coming to pay their respects. He was told later that his father had been a Holiness minister, but the only sign of that was a book that he found illustrated with pictures of the Devil and Hell. There was a particularly disturbing one of Death using a scythe to cut a person in half. Those images frightened him as a child, and would stay with him as he grew older.

"The only thing my father left my mother was a leather strap. It was like a barber strap – two inches wide and about a quarter of an inch thick with a hole in one end to hang on a nail on the wall. As I grew up I think that strap stayed on my backside more than it did on the nail," Thomas recalled.

When they arrived in Chase City his grandmother and Mr. Haskins let them move into their tiny, three room wooden shack. Thomas doesn't remember Mr. Haskins because he died shortly after they moved in, but he must have been a generous man because he had already taken in another grandchild, Margaret. She was the daughter of Eliza's sister who had died in childbirth, so the Haskins had been caring for her since she was a baby. "Don't ask me where everybody slept. We all crowded in there somehow, although we may have been sleeping on top of each other," he says.

Some homes in Chase City had electricity and indoor plumbing, but his grandmother's home had nei-ther. Of course they were not alone. Many people in that area were without those modern conveniences. A white family near his grandmother's was generous enough to allow them to share their well. Thomas used to take his wagon to their well, fill buckets with water, and bring them back to their house so his mother could wash their clothes and those that she started taking in to earn a little money.

Many people used oil lamps for light and had outdoor privies. But even their privy, or outhouse, was not up to the standards of most of the others. There were cracks in the walls, and it could be a breezy, chilly place to attend to one's business. Thomas says, "When you used it, you got the wind from all parts of the compass."

Small as his grandmother's house was, it was set in a haven of beauty and wonder for a young city boy who had grown up with paved streets and sidewalks. The little shack was surrounded by gardens and fruit trees, and nearby were fields of wildflowers and a forest.

His grandmother had a flower garden out front, and a vegetable garden in back of her shack. The vegetables she raised helped keep the family fed. By growing their own string beans, squash, and corn, they were able to stretch their meager food budget. When he got older, Thomas even had his own little plot to grow things, and he marveled at the miracle of how a tiny seed or grain of corn that was relatively soft could be planted in the dirt and then push its way up through the earth – even though the ground had hardened over it. And when that little seed become a plant, it gave them vegetables and flowers, or even trees. He thought that was miraculous, and seeing how things worked in nature was part of his spiritual education, and how he learned to embrace God for himself.

Thomas grew to love nature. He enjoyed walking through the forest and looking at the trees overhead. At times they almost seemed to whisper to him as the wind caused the leaves to rustle high above. There was also a creek to explore, and fields full of colorful wildflowers. No doubt about it, it was a glorious place for a child to grow up in, especially in the spring when the flowers and fruit blossoms filled the air with their fragrances. Just as the sweet fragrances surrounded their house, the mockingbird that sat in the walnut tree in front of the house filled the air with his song. The family woke to that mocking bird's song every morning.

But if they woke to the sounds of nature, they went to sleep to the sounds of the machinery not far away at the ice plant in town. It was a regular beat – thump, thump, thump, thump. It was always present, almost as if the little town had its own heartbeat.

Chase City is a small, sleepy town in Southwest Virginia. Dr. Rachel Dailey Hargrove was born and raised there in a family of twelve children. Her family was living there when Tom's mother brought her children to Chase City. At that time the population was around 1,800 – if you counted those in the graveyard. Today the population is almost 2,500.

As a child, Rachel tried to tag along with Thomas and two of her brothers. She says, "I used to try to hang with them, but they didn't really want me to. Thomas was a shy little kid, a little withdrawn, but full of mischief. He was around our house a lot because he was so close to my brother Roosevelt ('Rovel') and Charlie Irvin ('Cherry') - because he used to climb up his neighbors' cherry trees. Sometimes with their permission."

At one time Chase City was a busy tobacco market with farmers bringing their tobacco crops into the warehouses in the town each fall. There was a train stop, a Greyhound bus stop, a movie theater, a bank and the usual assortment of barber shops, drug stores, and other small shops. The main industry was a box factory, and many of the men worked there; but there was also a shirt factory where some of the black women got jobs.

The Great Depression and the drought that hit Southern Virginia around that time made life more difficult for the farmers in the area as tobacco prices tumbled. The Stock Market Crash of 1929 caused families all over the country to suffer great hardships as banks closed, including the one in Chase City. Life savings were wiped out, and many people lost their jobs. But to children like Thomas – or Tonnie as his friends called him – the Great Depression didn't mean much.

"Those were hard times, but we were accustomed to it. That was our natural state. All my early life was an economic depression as far as we were concerned. The Stock Market crash didn't bother us one little bit. But it was tough on the adults, I don't see how they made it, but they did," Thomas says matter of factly.

One way they survived was by bartering. "Sometimes neighbors would give us vegetables if they had extras of something. We grew corn, and I would take that corn and shell it, and then Ma would send me to the mill. I would take a bag of corn and swap it for a bag of cornmeal. We also had some chickens; and I used to go to one of the grocery stores to swap eggs for oil to use in our kerosene lamp. The couple that lived next to my grandmother's house was a whole lot better off than we were. They had pigs and cows, and they'd sell buttermilk to us at a price we could afford."

Rachel remembers those times well. "We were poor. You didn't realize how poor you were until you see what children have today, then you realize you were a very poor person. With 12 children at Christmastime we were happy to get apples and oranges. What would children today say if that was all they got for Christmas? But we had a lot of love, and I never went hungry. My mother was an excellent cook. She made her own bread and she used to make a lot of gravies, like liver gravy, so with that bread and all that gravy, you felt full. And if she had some cornbread or pudding when Thomas was around, she'd always send a little home to his grandmother."

Poor as they were, there was never any thought of begging. That was a disgrace. Kids would be disciplined for asking for money. "We earned what we got. The thing was to get a job, and do honest work." Even the young children did their part to bring a little money home to the family. In an early form of babysitting, some older black children were paid a nickel or so to play with young white children.

But most of the time they had fun. There was no money for toys, so they had to create their own. That brought out their imagination, developed their creativity, and gave them a sense of pride in what they could make themselves. Even though they didn't live in the best of circumstances, as long as they had food to eat, a roof over their heads, and friends to play with, they were happy – even if their clothes were hand-me-downs that had to be patched and mended.

There was one time when little Thomas was embarrassed because of his old clothes. He went to a birthday party wearing a pair of pants he had been given. He didn't realize that the pants were dry rotted, and that the seams were not very strong. While playing with the boys outside he bent over to kick a football, and then he heard a loud ripping sound and felt a little breeze behind him. Looking back he said he probably should have gone home then, but they hadn't served the refreshments yet, and he wasn't about to miss that. Someone found a safety pin and he pinned himself up, and his pants held together long enough for him to enjoy the ice cream and cake.

Although that incident was embarrassing, being poor was not something that was discussed. "As a child you don't know what poverty is unless someone tells you. I was so impressed by the things in nature that were around me that I found an excitement in life that no amount of money could give me. It's ironic that the time that was probably the hardest for my mother, and a lot of other people, was one of the happiest times in my life."

Neither of his brothers finished high school. Joe, the oldest, got as far as the ninth grade, but he left school when they left Richmond, and he and Ben got jobs in Chase City to support the family. Ben worked in sawmills and on farms, and Joe worked as a domestic at a white family's house. Joe did general work around the house and some cooking, which meant that sometimes he was able to bring leftover food home with him – a little chicken or some ice cream – that was something they all looked forward to. Ruth also worked as a domestic. When he was old enough, Thomas did what he could to earn money too. He'd pick wild berries - blackberries and dewberries - and go around to the homes in the white neighborhoods and sell them. Or course he'd save some for his mother, and those black-berries made mighty good tarts and pies.

His mother also used herbs and wild plants for cooking or home remedies. "My mother used to make a cough syrup by using the bark of a wild cherry tree, but I don't know what else she mixed with it, and I don't remember how potent it was or whether it worked or not, but that's the way it was in the country. People made a lot of what they used.

"We also drank sassafras tea all the time. There were little sassafras trees growing up out of the ground in certain places, and I would dig the roots up, and we would wash and clean them, and brew the roots in water on the stove. That was delicious to drink. There was also a bush called horse mint and we'd make tea out of that too, only we'd use the leaves for that tea. We also used to harvest a weed called watercress, or what we boys called 'creces salad.' It grew as a flat plant in low-lying places near the creek. We used to go down to the creek banks and cut bunches of that, and then Grandma or Ma would boil them like greens for supper. They were delicious, but it took a whole lot of them to make a potful."

In the '30s, like small towns all over the country, especially the South, Chase City was segregated. All of the stores on Main Street were owned and operated by whites, but there were shops and stores owned by Negroes scattered throughout the "colored" part of town. Negroes could shop wherever they wanted to, although they couldn't use the library, and they had to use the side door to enter the movie theater and then climb the stairs to sit in the balcony. As Rachel says, "It was a nice little town to grow up in, but you sort of knew your place. In that day and age there was no question about it. There were places that you could not go. You couldn't go into Garrett's Drug Store and get a soda and sit at the counter, you had to buy your soda and take it outside to drink it."

But that didn't bother little Thomas. "Garrett's was my favorite place in Chase City. I didn't care that I couldn't sit at the counter. I didn't go there for the sodas. I went there for the comic books. And when the comic books were outdated, Mr. Garrett would cut half the front cover off, and lower the price to a nickel. That's when I could buy them. I loved all those superheroes, Superman and Captain America, but the science fiction ones were my favorites – Buck Rogers and Flash Gordon – they were my heroes."

Although segregation was a way of life for the adults, it meant little to Thomas and his friends. Young black and white kids shot marbles together, played sand-lot football and baseball, jumped rope and played hop-scotch. "We had more things to do than we had daylight to do it in. I was fortunate to be born and reared in those times when children created most of the things we played with like our bows and arrows, slingshots, wag-ons, and scooters. And if we found some old car tires we would roll them and have races, or pile them on top of each other and climb down in there and have a little house. There was always lots of activity, and for the most part we got along fine. It wasn't until we got to be teen-agers that we stopped doing things together. By then most of the boys I hung around with were interested in girls. I was still playing cowboys and war games with my cousins who were younger than me, but the boys my age weren't interested in that anymore."

In Chase City even the adults got along pretty well, and there weren't any major racial incidents. Of course they had a jail, but there wasn't any real crime in the town – no murders, robberies, or muggings. Most of the people who occupied the jail were there because of fights, and those usually occurred on the weekends when people had been drinking and arguments broke out at some of the nightspots.

There were a couple of places blacks would hang out. Rachel says, "We called them cafes. Of course as kids we weren't allowed to go there, but we'd peek in the windows and watch the people dancing. In later days, we had two places; one was called the Red Door and the other was the Green Door. They were right next to each other. People would go up there on Saturday night, and go in one and get tired of that place, and leave and go next door. Eventually I think they got a beer license, but in those places they had bootleg liquor or people would bring a bottle with them as some people sold bootleg at their homes. But those were places that we knew children weren't supposed to go, and you'd better not be caught hanging around there. In those days children had a place, they weren't as free to speak and talk like they do now. Children had the utmost respect for adults, and if you didn't do what you were told, you knew you were going to get a butt whipping."

Once Rachel's brothers saved little Thomas from a sure butt whipping. Tom's older brother Ben had taught him how to fish, and he loved to fish in the creek. At one point Ben bought a large net with handles on each end. You would dip it in the water and scoop up a fish as you pulled it toward the bank. His mother told him not to touch that net, but one day when Rovel and Cherry came by to go fishing he couldn't resist the temptation and they took the net to the creek. They caught lots of fish and were going to split their catch three ways. But as they started up the dirt path to go home they saw his mother heading toward them. To Thomas the switch she was carrying looked like a peach tree on her shoulder. They heard her say, "Come and get it." The boys knew what that meant, so they decided to tell Thomas to keep all the fish. He had the fish behind his back and when they got right up to her, before she could say a thing, he swung the bucket full of fish in front of her. She was so surprised all she could say was, "Where did you get all those fish?" There were no more threats of discipline, and they had a wonderful fish dinner that night.

Fishing was just one of the things the boys enjoyed doing together. Rachel says, "They really got along very well together. They made their own entertainment. They built little scooters out of wheels and a piece of wood, and they made what we called grit shooters. They cut a Y-shaped branch of a small tree, and then they would cut a piece of rubber from an old inner tube or something, and put that on with string. They were like a slingshot, but we called them grit shooters because you used small rocks for the ammunition. Then they made wagons out of orange crates on old baby carriage wheels or skates. They'd sit in the box and ride down the hill. It was a little dangerous, but they liked to take a lot of chances."

Thomas got quite good with his slingshot. He used it to go hunting. Snakes, frogs, waterbugs – they all made good targets. He saw the older men hunt turkeys and squirrels, and so he hunted cardinals, mockingbirds, and goldfinches; they were his game. He used to take the birds he shot to an old woman who lived down the road from them, and she would pluck their feathers and cook them just like they were chicken.

The Cannons lived over the hill from the Daileys, Rachel's family, on West 3rd St. For a long time their street wasn't paved and it didn't have a name. "We were one of the last neighborhoods to get the streets paved and to get street lights."

The hill was called Craddock Hill, and there was an old abandoned house there. That house became the place Thomas would meet up with her brothers. It got to the point that when he would go to the Dailey house, Nannie Dailey, their mother, would put him to work while he waited for Rovel and Cherry. She'd give him a bucket and ask him to go to the well -which was about half a block away - and bring back some water. Thomas was just a skinny little kid, and that bucket was heavy when it was full of water. So to avoid fetching water whenever he wanted to play with his friends, they devised a signal. He would stand on top of the hill and give the signal, and then wait for them by the abandoned house.

Doc was one of Thomas's cousins, and he had another buddy called Popeye because somehow he had lost one eye. They were younger than the Dailey boys, but Tom played with them too, especially when Rovel and Cherry discovered girls and didn't have as much time for him as they once had.

One day Thomas's mother sent him to a field to cut straw so she could make a broom, and Doc and Popeye went along. For some reason that day Doc was wearing his father's rubber boots. Doc was just a little guy so while the boots came up to his father's knees, on him they came up to his hips. After he had cut a handful of straw, Thomas decided to tease the little boys and scare them, so he pulled a match out of his pocket and lit the straw. "My intention was to just let it blaze up a little bit, and I was dancing around and whooping it up, but a little breeze came up, and before I knew it the field caught on fire. We tried to stomp the fire out, and Popeye and Doc fought valiantly for a while, but then Doc saw it

26

was hopeless and said 'We'll be seeing you,' and they took off running. I was so amazed that Doc could run in those boots that I just stood there with fire all around me watching them go. It looked like the boots were carrying that little guy along."

A lady in a nearby house came out her back door and started screaming. The pigs in pens of the edge of the field started squealing, and then the fire started heading toward the woods. Eventually some local folks arrived and began to fight the fire. Then just as quickly as the breeze had come up, the wind turned. Like a miracle the fire went out before it got to the forest.

Sometimes after Thomas's mother would discipline him, he would go out and sit in the little corn crib behind the house and sulk. He'd think about running away, but then the aromas from the kitchen would start to waft out to the corn crib. He'd smell pork chops or potatoes frying and decide maybe things weren't so bad after all.

The white children in town went to the brick school in the middle of town, but the black children went to Chase City Graded School. From the Dailey house they would run across a little creek and up the hill to the school. It was a four-room wooden school that looked like a big white barn. There were four teachers, with one acting as principal and also teaching the 5th and 6th grades. The youngest children were in the primer grade, which was combined with the 1st grade.

27

Then another teacher taught the 2nd and 3rd grades, and another one taught the 4th grade. Each room had its own potbellied stove. Two rooms were on the east side of a wide hall and two rooms were on the west. The hall was used for devotionals and special programs like hygiene. There was a little sink there with running water, and the teachers showed them how to wash hands properly using Lifebuoy soap. And every day before starting the lessons, the teacher would inspect them for cleanliness by checking their hands, ears, and teeth. The children scrambled to fix themselves up before each inspection.

The east side of the school rested on a foundation near the ground, but the west side was elevated on pillars, and that's where the coal was kept to fuel the stoves. The pillars were tall enough that students could walk under there to collect coal in the scuttle and carry it into the classroom. Thomas liked that chore. "We boys loved to be assigned to bring in the coal or take out the ashes. That was a prime assignment because our classmates would be inside struggling with their books, and we were out in the fresh air. Sometimes we'd even get in a few games of marbles under there before we took the coal back in the school. The teacher thought we were out being so good and working away digging coal, and there we were shooting marbles."

Some boys volunteered to come early and get the fires in the stoves started, but often when it was time for classes the room wasn't warm enough. "The teacher would gather all the pupils around the pot bellied stove and she'd put the smaller children up in her lap and rub their feet to get the circulation going. Some of those kids walked miles to school, and some of those smaller kids had really cold feet. As soon as that old stove started perkin' and the room got warmer we'd move back farther from it. Eventually the whole room was warm, then you'd go to your seat and your studies. But that was great because it gave it kind of a homey atmosphere – as if the teacher was the mother and we were her children. That drew us all close together."

But the pot-bellied stove was also used as a disciplinary instrument. There was no dunce stool in the corner where someone would sit with a pointed hat on his head if he misbehaved; instead they had to sit on a stool near the pot-bellied stove. "When that old stove turned cherry red, it could be very uncomfortable on that stool. The teacher would let whoever had misbehaved sit there until he was probably about two minutes from a heat stroke, and then she'd let him go back to his seat. That form of punishment worked because nobody wanted to get that hot seat. And she had good instincts about when they'd had enough, because I don't remember her losing a single child that way."

The only unpleasant incident he remembers from school was that somebody wrote something negative about one of the teachers on the outhouse wall, and he got blamed for it. He used to draw cartoons, and because he did those little drawings, that made him a prime suspect. Then one of his classmates told the teacher it looked like his handwriting, and that did it. As far as the teachers were concerned, he was guilty. The writing did look a little bit like his, but he didn't do it. His teacher even isolated him in the closet for a while, and then brought in his first-grade teacher, and she tried to talk him into confessing. He maintained his innocence, because he didn't know anything about it, and hadn't even known the graffiti was out there until the teacher took him out to see it. They couldn't get him to confess, and they finally forgot about it. But he never got that off his mind and years later, after he was married, he visited that teacher and brought up that incident. She remembered it, and he found out that a boy who had been in his class had confessed that his brother, who was older and didn't go to the elementary school, had written the message with his left hand, and somehow that made it look like Thomas's writing.

When children completed the sixth grade at Chase City, they went on to Thyne Institute. Thyne was one mile out of town, and in the morning you could see all the black kids walking up the railroad tracks to school. It was a private school established in 1876 by the United Presbyterian Church of Pittsburgh, PA. to educate the recently freed slaves.

Rachel went to Thyne and remembers that they

had teachers from all over. Some were white, and some were black. The principal was from Ohio. It was a boarding school and they had boys and girls dormitories because students also came there from out of state because it was known for quality education. It cost 50 cents a month to attend.

By the time he left the elementary school, Thomas's brother Joe had gotten married and moved away from home, so it was up to Ben, Ruth, and him to provide for their mother. He started the seventh grade at Thyne, but they just couldn't afford the tuition in addition to the cost of books and other expenses, so he dropped out after the first half of the year and began to work.

He still credits those teachers at Chase City Graded School with giving him a good educational foundation, and his mother with instilling good values in him. "That's where the foundation for my life was laid. The values and strong work ethic I learned in Chase City helped me later in life. My mother taught me to live by the Golden Rule, but most important of all she and my brothers gave me the tools I needed to succeed in life. I am what I am because they were what they were, and I'm forever indebted to them for the principles and character they taught me."

Chapter 3

A Student's Plight

June 27, 2003

Dear Mr. Millsaps,

Once again I must call upon you and the Richmond Times-Dispatch to lend a helping hand. I wish to respond to an article I've just read in the morning paper. It is entitled: "Hungry for education." It was written by Staff Writer Michael Martz and it details the story of a recent graduate of Hermitage High School from Afghanistan, Sayed Hashmat Saddat.

This young man is a giant among men. He has survived tragedy, trials and tribulations that would have crushed the spirit of lesser mortals and caused them to throw up their hands in despair and defeat. Instead, Sayed's troubles seem merely to have fired his fierce determination to get an education and to render service to others. His heartbreaking ordeal made him reach deep within himself for the spiritual resources and strength to enable him to reach for the stars in pursuit of his dreams.

Sayed Hashmat Saddat is a magnificent, highly-courageous young man who is surely deserving of the $1,000 check I have enclosed for him to use as he pleases. Perhaps he may wish to use some of this money toward helping to further his education Hopefully, this little monetary gift will inspire him to "stay the course."

As it was Mr. Michael Martz, the staff writer, who precipitated this gift with his article, I would appreciate it if he will present the check to Mr. Saddat for me.

I applaud the Catholic Diocese of Richmond for its Refugee and Immigration Services program which has helped to resettle so many needy and deserving immigrants here in our area and helped them to rebuild their lives and realize their dreams in our democrat-

ic society.

Also I am grateful to the editors and staff of the Richmond Times-Dispatch for continuing to bring their stories to me. Thanks a Thousand!

Very cordially yours,
Tom Cannon

When Sayed Hashmat Saddat entered Hermitage High School, his classmates thought he was a little strange – maybe even crazy. Not because he was from Afghanistan, didn't like McDonald's hamburgers, or spoke with an accent, but because he loved school. Hashmat also wondered why the students did not appreciate the education they were offered in this country, and why they did not show their teachers more respect.

Hashmat says, "I love to learn. When I came here I was so impressed by the facilities and the technology. Everything was of the highest quality. Students had i-Book laptop computers, there was a biology lab, and a large auditorium. It was so different from how we learned in Afghanistan. Our schools and books were almost destroyed by war."

During the war in Afghanistan the soldiers burned all the chairs and tables from the schools to keep themselves warm during the winter. Hashmat remembers that they even took the wooden frames from the windows and burned them. As he says, "Almost everything was destroyed, the economy, education, construction – nothing was left. There were no publishing companies to publish books, so if we had a textbook we had to share it. One student would take it home for one night, then another for another night. It was usually three students to one book.

"I was very bothered when I saw the American students were not behaving in class, and some students didn't use the i-Books they were given properly. That is a wonderful tool to learn, and some students just downloaded music and looked at movies. They used it like a TV. Children are dying for education in Afghanistan, and most other countries in Asia. When I see the wonderful facilities here, and that the students don't appreciate them, that bothers me a lot," he says.

Hashmat spent one and a half years at Hermitage. He began as a junior, but after about four months he was promoted to the senior class. His favorite subjects were math and biology, both interested him immensely. He enjoyed every day in class studying those subjects. He also studied advanced computer networking software operations at Hermitage Technical Center, a three-credit, college-level class which normally takes two years to complete, but he finished it in one year. He graduated from Hermitage with a 3.75 grade point average, and was also awarded the Jefferson Cup for community service.

When Hashmat first came here and people learned that he was from Afghanistan, he endured questions like if he knew bin Laden. "People would say things like, 'Have you met bin Laden? Have you shaken his hand?' I would laugh and say, 'Look guys, you people get to watch TV here whenever you want to. The Taliban closed down our TV stations and if a family was reported to have a TV, they would show up, break the TV and punish the family. So you have seen him before me, because I haven't seen his picture in Afghanistan.' When I came here to the United States, I saw his picture on TV. I was just an ordinary citizen, a civilian, and we didn't know the man. I'm sorry to say I don't believe the media here really expresses all the true facts to the people. And people, even my teachers, thought that everybody in Afghanistan likes war, and I was telling them 'No, we don't like war.' One person even said 'I hear that the religion of Islam teaches people to blow themselves up for God's blessing.' I told her that was not true. Islam is not a religion of violence and war. It is a religion of love, peace, and most importantly, justice. It is the extremists that teach the wrong things. I would like people to understand that Muslims are not terrorists. There isn't any religion to teach destroying humanity. It is said in Islam, 'If you save one life you save humanity, if you kill one soul you kill humanity.' And they said 'Oh, Hashmat, it's so nice to know from another person's perspective.'"

Another misconception that Hashmat has tried to correct is that contrary to what many Americans believe, people from Afghanistan do not consider themselves Arabs or Middle Easterners. They are Central Asians or South Asians.

Hashmat's parents died in Afghanistan many years ago, and he and his six siblings and aunt fled to Pakistan because of persecution toward people in general. They came to the United States and settled in Virginia with the help of the Catholic Diocese of Richmond. Reading Michael Martz's story, and learning how Hashmat was now helping others who come to the States from Afghanistan or Iran compelled Tom to send him a check.

Jane Mendenhall of the Catholic Diocese says, "Hashmat was the spokesman for his family because he was fluent in English. We were incredibly grateful that he spoke English as well as he did, and we have used his skill in English translation since he got here to help other families. He told me he studied English in Afghanistan and Pakistan and enjoyed it. He is incredibly motivated and is also very intelligent. He is an exceptional young man, and he really wanted to give back to the community."

Hashmat can translate for people from Afghanistan who speak Dari as well as people from Iran who speak Farsi as they are basically the same languages. He began translating for new arrivals as soon as he was settled in Richmond. He translated for families when they went to job interviews and job orientation programs. Sometimes he helped with medical appointments, took people to the doctor and translated for them when they were there. He made phone calls for those who couldn't speak English, and also helped get children settled in school.

Hashmat says, "I also volunteer and help people who come to Richmond through the Virginia Counsel of Churches. When I came here, I needed help. So I understand that it is really hard for some people. Now I try the best that I can to help people. Once there was a refugee family and one of the children was having some difficulties in school. He didn't know English and didn't understand the teacher and didn't feel like he fit in. So I gave him myself for an example and I said, 'Things change, I found some friends.' I encouraged him just as my mentor John Daily with Grace Community Baptist Church encouraged me. I was inspired to help others in the community by Mr. Daily and my own belief in humanity."

Once, Hashmat took a young man from Afghanistan who had only been in Richmond for two or three months to the Department of Motor Vehicles because he wanted to get a driver's license. Hashmat translated the driver's manual for him and helped the man get a learner's permit.

Although Hashmat says learning the English language is probably the biggest problem for new refugees, he also says that understanding the laws and getting accustomed to the food are also problems. "In Afghanistan anybody who had a gun was a king, and they could do almost anything they wanted."

He still has not gotten accustomed to American food and doesn't like hamburgers or sandwiches. He was surprised by some of the things students at Hermitage ate for lunch, like chips and fries, as he didn't think they were very healthy. He usually had some rice, beans, and meat or chicken. He says Afghans spend more time cooking things, and he doesn't like frozen or fast food. At first they had trouble with the rice most people buy in the grocery store, because it wasn't the type of rice they were used to. Eventually they found an Indian grocery store that carries rice that is similar to what they had in Afghanistan, and now they do a lot of their grocery shopping there.

To be able to make all these adjustments while helping other people takes a very special person, and Mendenhall says that Hashmat is representative of a lot of refugees who come here with literally nothing and succeed.

She says, "It's a very moving story. He lost his parents, and then came to a new country and has worked very hard to succeed and take care of his own family, as well as to help others. We're very proud of him, and appreciate Mr. Cannon's generous donation to him."

Reading Michael Martz's story, and learning how Hashmat was now helping other Afghans who come to the Richmond area from different countries compelled Tom Cannon to send him a check. He wanted to give Hashmat an extra "pat on the back" because he came to the United States under such difficult circumstances, and worked so hard to get his education. His check also served as a good will gesture to show Hashmat that not all Americans are hostile to Afghans and other Muslims. Tom feels that since the tragedy of 9/11 there is a lot of animosity and hostility in this country towards people of Arab descent, because most of the terrorists were Arabs. He says, "That event aroused anger and hostility towards all Arab-Americans, and most of them were as innocent and shocked about the terrorist acts as we were. I was concerned about the friendly, law-abiding, Arab-American citizens. So in addition to being a gesture to boost Hashmat's morale and confidence in his new country, I was hoping other Arab citizens would read about this gift and know they are not hated by everybody in this country."

Michael Marts delivered Tom's $1,000 check to Hashmat. When he did he explained that Tom Cannon was not a rich man, but a man who retired from the postal service and gave checks to people he had read about in the newspaper who had done something special. He told him that Cannon had chosen him because he worked so hard for his education, and was now doing humanitarian work.

"When he gave me that $1,000 check, I couldn't believe it," says Hashmat. He asked for Tom's address and wrote him a thank you note on a postcard that was from Afghanistan. "I thanked him very much, and in response to his generosity I pray for him to be healthy all the time. I said how much of an inspiration his gift was. This was not only $1,000 for me, but it was a very big lesson as well. I learned from him, and I pray to God to make me able to walk in his shoes one day. I hope to buy a personal computer for my studies at J. Sergeant Reynolds Community College where I will study computer science, and his money will help me with that."

Hashmat had originally wanted to be a pilot, but the tragic events of the Sept. 11th terrorist attack affected those plans. "My ambition was to learn to fly and be a commercial pilot. I came to the USA very soon after Sept. 11 happened. It was such a bad thing, and my people are suspected of that. So I didn't know how I could learn to fly. My school guidance counselor said one option is to join the Army. I said 'I have memories from my country because the war was so horrible,' and I said 'I'm a peace-loving person, and I hate war and bloodshed, and I would hate to be involved in the Army.'"

Then he had an idea and got an appointment with a recruiting officer. One of his American acquaintances went with him, and Hashmat explained that he didn't want to be involved in fighting, but that if there were a non-combative section that helped people he would like to do that. He thought as a pilot he could help rescue people from disasters, either natural or man-made. But the recruiter explained that even in a non-combative unit in time of war you might have to carry weapons and supplies to the battlefield.

Hashmat says, "I couldn't do that. I love people, and I believe in humanity. As a Muslim that's my religion, so I don't want anything to do with the Army if it is supporting killing people or a war, even indirectly."

Chapter 4

The Navy

Thomas Cannon, 1942 (Navy Photo)

Smoke was still rising from parts of the field as "General Tonnie" placed the World War I helmet on his head and led his soldiers Popeye and Doc in a charge through the battlefield. War was a game the young boys relished, and the field where the dust from the sawmill was burnt made a perfect place to play. To them it was a smoldering battlefield with enemy troops hiding in the dips and depressions. "I was the general because I was bigger than my little buddies. The boys my size and age were chasing girls by then, and they left me behind in the dust. I was still playing games, and they were dressing up and chasing girls."

Eventually childhood games had to be put aside when he dropped out of Thyne High School at thirteen and went to work. He had a variety of jobs. One of his main jobs was with a local grocer. The grocer had a contract with the train depot to deliver Western Union telegrams, so he rode his bike all over town delivering either groceries or telegrams. He also caddied at the golf club. He did whatever work he could find to earn money.

He gave most of his money to his mother to help support the family, but sometimes he used a little of it to make a visit to Richmond to see his brother Joe and his wife, Nellie. On one of those visits he met a young girl who lived about a half a block away who had become friends with Nellie. Her name was Princetta, a pretty name for a pretty little girl, but she was only eleven and he was just fourteen so he didn't have romantic feelings towards her — not then. At that time he just enjoyed seeing her whenever he visited his brother.

He also made enough money to buy his family a large radio. It cost $15, and was a big purchase for him so he put it on layaway at the department store, and gradually paid it off. Up until then he had been listening to the crystal radio that his friend Otis Hepburn had shown him how to make. Otis was the only one of his buddies who liked electronics, and he studied *Popular Science* magazine like Tom studied the comics. Otis showed him how to take a crystal that was about the size of a grain of corn and looked like a piece of metal, and hook one end of a coil of wire to that crystal, and the other to a set of headphones and make a radio. They ordered the crystal and headphones from a mail order catalogue, along with other things like model airplanes that the boys enjoyed making. But the crystal set amazed Tom. By rubbing a little copper wire that they called a cat whisker across the surface, local stations could be heard — he even got WCAU in Philadelphia. The only problem with the crystal set was that you didn't have control over the stations, they tended to fade in and out. When he was able to bring the big radio home, they listened to the music of the big bands and programs like *First Line,* which featured stories about the Navy and naval battles in the early days of World War II.

When Tom was around sixteen, war became a reality for the United States. It was no longer just a program on the radio or a game played with cap guns in sawdust fields. The Japanese bombing of Pearl Harbor changed all that. After December 7, 1941, he and his friends wanted to get into the action for real.

But Tom was too young, all he could do was listen from the side porch of Silone Baptist Church as the mayor held one of his town meetings to explain how the war would effect Chase City and its inhabitants. Blackouts, food and gasoline rationing – these would all become part of daily life.

The National Guard was called up and replaced by a unit of the Virginia Protective Force, which was like a civilian militia. It was stationed at the armory right in the center of town on Main Street along with recruiters for the Army and Navy. Some of Tom's older friends signed up, and he wished he could go off to defend his country too. He says, "I remember the night the troop train came through Chase City to pick up the local National Guard to take them to camp. There was a big crowd of people all around the train depot seeing these Chase City National Guardsmen off. We were all really caught up in the war spirit that night."

Patriotism was deeply instilled in the students during their years at Chase City Graded School. In the grades between primer and the 6th grade their classroom teachers instilled patriotism in them. They said the Pledge of Allegiance every day, and there were flags everywhere. They had patriotic recitations and patriotism was very much a part of the curriculum and study program.

"That's why I was so gung-ho to go to war," he says. "I could just envision myself on the deck of a destroyer being a hero in combat at sea. Patriotism was also part of our lives because back then our heroes were comic book characters who were great defenders of America. I remember one character that was particularly popular, Captain America. That comic book was very popular, so our heroes - both real and imaginary - were defending America. I grew up as a real 'red, white, and blue patriot', and ready for action."

Then word spread around town that they were hiring construction workers at the new Army camp that was being built not far from Chase City. A bus came to town each morning and picked up the workers and transported them out to the site of the future Camp Pickett.

"Several of us boys lied on the application form and said we were eighteen rather than sixteen, or seventeen. But they were paying good money, and for us it was a matter of survival as well as a way of helping the war effort." He says, "We jacked our age up a couple of years and went to work at Camp Pickett. They knew I wasn't eighteen, I was just a little, bitty skinny guy, and more the size of an average twelve year old boy, so they knew I wasn't eighteen, but they were desperate for laborers at that time because all the young men were going into the military. We worked right alongside the big men building the base hospital. Some of those men resented it because we were making the same money as they were, but we were doing the same work – digging ditches and trenches for the foundations, pushing wheelbarrows of concrete, lifting heavy lumber, all that goes into constructing a building from the ground up. We did our job, and did it well.

"Finally I got a break from digging ditches. They gave me a job as water boy. I carried a tank on my shoulders full of water, and I'd go around with paper cups to give all the working men a drink of water. That was much lighter, easier work. So I got a real break that way."

Shortly after he turned seventeen, Tom persuaded his mother to sign permission papers to let him join the Navy even though he wasn't eighteen. Alfred Carter was another of his close buddies, and Alfred's brother had joined the Navy, and then Alfred did, so Tom decided to follow them into the Navy, too. None of them knew that the Navy was segregated when they signed up. Tom had no way of knowing that his dream of serving on a warship was still impossible at that point in time. The seaman's branch was opened to black personnel early in 1942, and he read about that in the *Pittsburgh Courier* – one of the newspapers that were available in Chase City. That paper printed news from the new Great Lakes Naval Training Center. They had pictures showing blacks at the Camp Robert Smalls training area, a part of the Great Lakes Training Center that was named after a black Naval officer in the Civil War.

Up until that time, a black enlistee was classified as a steward's mate, which meant being an officer's steward, a mess attendant or a cook. Thomas was under the impression that as a member of the seaman's branch he would be able to serve on a warship. He says, "That's what fooled me. I wanted to serve on a ship, but the Navy used the black personnel in the service battalions – work details. They were essential, too. Somebody had to do that work, but I might have gone into some other branch of service if I had known that. But they were all pretty much the same. The Marines didn't put black Marines into fighting units either. They were at supply depots loading and unloading boxcars and stuff like that, just like we were. It was pretty much the same thing throughout the military. There was rigid segregation – that was the law of the land. But I went into the Navy thinking that I would be going to sea on a warship, and I wouldn't have gone into the Navy if I had known that option wasn't open to me."

He signed up with the Navy in Chase City, but went to Richmond to be sworn in. There he met the other men who would be in the group with him going to the Great Lakes Naval Training Center. One of them, Sam Graveley would become the first black admiral in the Navy.

Tom was not big and not particularly athletic. He was a seventeen-year-old kid away from home for the first time. With the war raging on, he knew there was always danger in the military. He remembered those frightening pictures of Death and Hell that he had seen when he was a child, and hearing people talk about eternal damnation if you died without being baptized. So when he was going through boot camp at Great Lakes, he decided to ask the Chaplain to baptize him. He thought, "Heck, I might as well let this Navy Chaplain baptize me. It can't do any harm, and might do some good because I'm going into a shooting war soon, and I need all the help I can get."

The Chaplain made the arrangements to baptize him, but Tom had a few issues with the plan to baptize him in the Navy base swimming pool without doing anything to purify the water. "Those Navy guys were going into Chicago on liberty, and drinking and carousing around, patronizing houses of ill repute, and then coming back to base and jumping into the pool. I would think the swimming pool water was spiritually polluted, and I would have thought the Chaplain should have said something, or done something – maybe a little ritual – to purify the water before he dipped me under it. I would rather he had baptized me in Lake Michigan, but it was late fall and too cold for that. So after the ceremony where he dipped me in the shallow end, he swam down to the deep end of the pool and got out. I didn't follow him. I couldn't swim that well, and my faith wasn't quite as strong as his, so I climbed out of the shallow end. But for the record – I was baptized."

When he arrived at boot camp he was absolutely broke. He didn't have a penny, and it was three weeks before he received his first paycheck. His first check was for the grand sum of $15. His mother thought he was making a lot of money, and she wrote him asking him to send her some. By then his sister Ruth had given birth to a child and had left him with their mother, so she needed the money to pay for the care of the child. Eventually Thomas had an allotment made out to her, so she had a regular income.

When their class graduated from Camp Robert Smalls, most of the men were assigned to Port Chicago in California. Tom lost track of Sam Gravely as he went on to a different posting, but he followed his career and was proud of having gone through boot camp with a man who was to achieve so many firsts for blacks in the Navy.

Thomas spent his first Christmas in the military at Port Chicago. It was an ammunition depot where huge, gray ships were loaded down with bombs, grenades – all the types of ammunition needed for the weapons at the front lines. Some of the men worked on the dock taking the ammunition out of boxcars and putting it into nets to be hoisted up onto the ships and down into the holds. Others were unloading the ammunition and storing it in the ship for the voyage. The loading and unloading was fairly routine. All you had to do was lift the boxes up or roll the bombs into the nets, and not drop anything. The men who had the hard jobs were the winch operators who had to lift the nets up from the dock, swing them over the ship, and lower them down into the hold. From their seat up on top of the winch, their vision of the dock was obscured. They depended on the hatch tender to guide them with hand signals. He stood over at the side of the ship and looked down onto the dock and used hand signals to tell the operator when to lower the net or hoist it up.

During their off time, a couple of the men made some signal flags and began to send each other semaphore signals. Tom and others would watch from the barracks windows and laugh at these guys out there waving their arms around like silly symphony conductors. But Tom enjoyed learning new things, and soon became intrigued with the signalmen. He took an old pair of denim jeans and cut them up and made squares, nailed them to some pieces of wood, and made his own flags. He and shipmate Samuel Powell got a copy of a book with the signal letters and began practicing themselves. They became so involved with signaling that they decided they wanted to take the test to become signalmen.

"I have to give credit to the administrators of Port Chicago because they had some little devices made for us to practice Morse code with at night. They were like little signal guns. These were unconventional little gadgets, but they served the purpose because all you need is a blinking light. You can practice Morse code with a flashlight. And they put up a flagpole and they bought us a set of international flags that they fly on ships at sea, but we didn't have any manual to tell us how to use them. They were helping us along in a small way, but they wouldn't let us go to signal school. They said we would have to become signalmen first. Of course that didn't make any sense. If we were signalmen then we wouldn't have any need to go to signal school.

"Eventually we got to go over to Treasure Island to get tested to see if we could pass the signalman's test. We did fine with the signal flags – knew our semaphore signals perfectly, but then the chief signalman testing us asked us about the signal flags used by the war ships and we didn't have a clue. We had no books on how warships used those flags. The white chief signalman who was giving us the test was angry that they would let us come there to take the examination knowing we didn't know about the other half of the test – the written examination on the flags. So he gave us the books that we needed to study, and he said that when we felt that we were ready we should notify him, and he would have us back over to take the written half of the exam. That's what we did, and we went back and took the exam."

Tom had also requested to be sent to gunnery school.

That request was granted, and an order came in for him to be sent to the Naval Gunnery School at Point Montara, California, a considerable distance from Port Chicago, for a three-day training period in July of 1944. While he was gone, there was a horrible accident. At 10:20 the night of July 17, two of the vessels being loaded at Port Chicago exploded killing all the men at the scene. The SS *Quinault Victory* and SS *E.A. Bryan* were both destroyed, and there was considerable damage to the dock area. At least 350 men were killed, including some civilians. All of Tom's friends and buddies were gone, including Samuel Powell. Nobody knew the exact cause of the accident. An extensive investigation failed to provide more details about the mysterious accident

"Port Chicago was a major landmark in my life. It might have led me to feel that I was saved because I had a mission to do. It started some very deep thinking and made me wonder how fate determines who will live and who will die on any occasion." It would not be the last time he wondered if there might be something ahead that he was to accomplish.

Shortly after the explosion, Tom's promotion to Signalman 3rd Class was posted on the bulletin board, as was Sam Powell's.

Some of the men who were asked to continue loading ammunition refused to do so, citing safety concerns after the explosion. Their mutiny brought to light the fact that many of the black men who had joined the

Navy were led to believe that they would get the same sea duty assignments that the white sailors did. Those men who refused to load ammunition were charged with mutiny and convicted, even though they were defended by the famous NAACP lawyer Thurgood Marshall. Tom didn't agree with their mutinous actions. "I didn't like that work myself as I had hoped to go to sea on a warship. But looking back on it, we had it made working there. It was gravy compared to the men fighting for their lives in the Pacific. We got three hot meals a day, after eight hours we got to sleep on clean sheets, we had a recreation center with a pool, a barbershop, and plenty of liberty to go to San Francisco. Some of the sailors who were married were even living with their families off-base. So you couldn't beat that. I'm sure some of those white sailors would have been happy to trade places with us. We weren't being shot at. Nobody was dropping bombs on us. I knew the danger. Every time we went down to load the ship, I knew it could be the last time, but I worried more about the sailors who had to sail across the Pacific Ocean to the war zone with a ship full of ammunition with Japanese submarines in the water ready to attack them. I'll defend the Navy on that point. It was essential to get that ammunition to the war zone where the men were fighting. It was a critical and valuable job. The U.S. forces in the Pacific couldn't fight if they didn't have the ammunition. Our work had been going on smoothly and efficiently from the very beginning. There weren't any problems or complaints at that base until after the accident."

Tom's next assignment was the U.S. Naval Net Depot at Tiburon, California. That was a depot that controlled the submarine nets across the harbor just inside the Golden Gate Bridge. There was a floating section of the submarine net attached to cables and two net gate vessels, the YNG 18 and the YNG 20 that opened and closed the nets.

Large, lumbering ships would signal to enter or leave the harbor. If it was daylight and they could see each other, they would use their signal flags or signal lights using Morse code. But they often had to cut through the infamous San Francisco fog. The ships would rely on their foghorn for communication. "They had a certain series of blasts on their horn that would let us know they wanted to go out, or in some cases that a ship wanted to come in. But they couldn't pass by until we opened that section of the submarine net between the two small gate vessels. The YNG 18 would pull the floating net gate over to our side, which would open the channel and the ship would sail between us. Then when they were through, the YNG18 would signal the YNG20 to close the gate, and their winch would pull the gate back across the channel. Our vessels were close enough where we could use the signal lights, but sometimes we couldn't see the ship that was sailing between us until they were right on top of us. You'd look up and

it looked like a whole mountain was coming down on
you. That was frightening, these great big aircraft carriers or battleships looming up out of the fog. I escaped
injury there too because I started on the YNG18 and
was sent to the YNG20. When I was on the YNG20 a
ship crashed into the 18. Then I was sent back to the 18
and a ship hit the 20. I was just a hop, skip, and a jump
ahead of disaster, but fortunately no one was hurt in
either accident."

In 1945 black members of the seamen's branch began
to be assigned to sea duty. Many, like Tom, were assigned
to service ships, transports, oilers, and supply ships that
were serving the war ships. Tom was assigned to the
USS Niobrara, a supply ship that provided fuel oil for the
warships. It was one of a group of oilers attached to the
Third Fleet. The war had ended in Europe, and naval
ships were assembling in the Caroline Islands for an all-
out invasion of Japan. They were midway between Pearl
Harbor and the Caroline Islands when they got word
that the atomic bomb had been dropped and the war
was essentially over.

"I don't remember discussions onboard ship about
what the atomic bomb was. It was a mystery to us, but
everybody was happy the war was over. From the
Caroline Islands, the Third Fleet then sailed to take up
occupation duty in Tokyo Bay," remembered Tom.

It was on the *Niobrara* that he encountered racial problems. He and another black signalman, John Wesley Wade,

were assigned to the ship, and they were the first members of the black seaman's branch to serve on that ship.

As a signalman he was a member of the gang which manned the bridge of the ship. It was where the ship's movements were controlled, and the radiomen and sonar men were also stationed there. "All the signalmen were white except for the two of us. Wade had gone to signal school. I was the only one that I knew of who ever became a signalman without going to signal school."

The other duties on the ship were carried out by the deck gang which handled the lines that tied up the ships that came alongside to take on fuel oil, and they were also the ones who swabbed the decks.

"All the members of the deck crew were white Southerners and many of them were extremely bitter and angry at our being assigned to their ship as signalmen. They were very hostile towards us. Some of them even said they would mutiny before they worked with us. Now, they had blacks on there, but they were cooks, mess attendants, and stewards' mates; not men assigned to the bridge. One of the white sailors told me they just came from the China Sea, and they weren't going to take any stuff from us. He said some of them would stick a knife in you in a minute. I said, 'We didn't come on here to start any problems. We're not going to start any problems, but we're not going to run from them either. We were assigned to your ship and if you have any objections, you object to the people that assigned us here.' Once they became accustomed to us, they saw we were just like anyone else and did our jobs, that's when we began to feel accepted."

The first time Tom went into the galley he took his tray and sat down at the table with some of his white shipmates. "All of them grabbed up their trays and walked off to another table. So after that happened I deliberately went to the other end of the galley and sat down with my back to them to eat my food – to let them know it didn't mean anything to me to eat with them – the food didn't taste any better. But I wasn't going to segregate myself to begin with, I was going to try to fit in with the crew, but when I saw that they did-n't want to eat with me I wasn't going to push myself on them."

Race came up again one night when Tom was com-municating with the signalman on a cruiser anchored nearby. When it was quiet and there was nothing to do, signalmen often signaled those on another ship even though they couldn't see each other. On this occasion after asking where Tom had been serving, Tom respond-ed that he had mostly had land duty loading ships. The other signalman responded that he thought most of the land duty went to *boogies*. Tom signaled back, *What are boogies?* The other signalman sent back, *You know, niggers.* Tom signaled back. *I am a Negro.* He said, "That light shut down so fast – I guess he didn't know there were any black signalmen in the Navy then."

The *Niobrara* arrived in Tokyo Bay some weeks before VJ Day, and they were still in the area when the surrender was signed on the *USS Missouri*. He was with a group of men standing on the fantail of the ship observing the ceremony with binoculars. They saw the boats taking Japanese officials to the ship and saw them sign the documents. They also heard the radio coverage of the event and were amused when the radio announcer embellished his description of the event by saying, *As soon as the last signature was affixed to the surrender document the sun which had been absent all day suddenly burst through the clouds as if to symbolize a bright new day of peace on earth.* Tom said, "That was probably one of the biggest lies he ever told. When he said the sun came out, we all groaned and laughed too. Maybe the sun was shining somewhere else on earth, but it wasn't shining over Tokyo Bay that day."

At one point Tom was given a pass to go into Tokyo. He and some other members of the crew went into a store and nearly frightened the owner and his family to death. "We were just there to buy some souvenirs, but they didn't know what we wanted. I guess we were the first servicemen they had seen close up, and they had probably never seen a black man. I bought some things, including a doll for Princetta, because I had been corresponding with her, and thought she might like a souvenir of Japan."

Shortly after that he was returned to the States for discharge. On the way home the ship swerved suddenly, and all the men lost their balance for a minute. He learned that the ship had swerved to avoid a mine floating in the water, and he felt he had been spared from death once again.

After arriving on the West Coast, he traveled across the country by train to Camp Shelton to the Navy's separation center in Virginia near Norfolk. "Of course before we were separated they gave us a chance to re-up. I wasn't about to re-up. I wanted out. Many of the first group of black naval officers were resigning, and that seemed to alarm the Navy so they became a little more open and tolerant. After all, they had spent a lot of money training these men and they were not staying in the Navy, so things changed."

But things took longer to change in the civilian world as Tom found out when he went to buy a bus ticket to his brother's house in Richmond. He was standing in the ticket line at the Greyhound Bus Station in Norfolk, and a black man came running up to him and grabbed him by the arm and said, "Come on, you can't buy a ticket here. You have to go behind the booth to buy your ticket." Then when he was on the bus and it stopped at a roadside rest stop, the black servicemen who were on that bus couldn't be served at that restaurant. They had to go about a block away to get drinks and snacks from a vending machine at a gas station.

"I was finally waking up to the reality of our great democracy and beginning to see it all as a big sham. I became very bitter – *but with the system, never with the race of white people.* I can't conceive of anybody hating a race of people because of the conduct of a relative few. It was the Jim Crow system that was sanctioned by the U.S. Government that embittered me so much. It took a while, and it was a gradual process to get rid of those feelings. I'll always be grateful to the two newspapers in Richmond at that time, the *Times-Dispatch* and the *News Leader* for helping me to outgrow that feeling of anger towards the system. They allowed me to vent my rage through letters to the editor. As the years went by the letters became less hostile, and I got over those feelings."

Chapter 5

Patriotism

In 1974, the following letter was sent to the governor of each state regarding the 200th birthday of the United States, the Bicentennial Celebration.

Dear Sir:

Before attempting to explain what this letter is, I feel that the first necessity is to explain what it is NOT. It is not a "publicity stunt." It is not a "promotional gimmick." It is not a "scheme" designed to curry favor with any social or political faction in your state or in any other.

This letter along with the enclosed postal money order is simply one man's tribute to this great nation, the United States of America, in observance of her forthcoming birthday of July 4, 1976. This historic occasion, the Bicentennial Celebration, has been selected as the most propitious time projection in which I best can express my sincere appreciation to this nation and the people thereof for all they have done for me and meant to me as a citizen and World War II veteran.

As a method of expressing said appreciation, I have chosen to send a United States postal money order in the amount of fifty dollars ($50.00) to each state in the Union.

Collectively, the fifty dollars represent a salute to the specific state addressed; but individually each dollar therein represents one of the fifty states of which the United States of America is composed. Thus does the fifty dollars serve as a symbolic reminder of "one for all and all for one." Therefore this gift is to be regarded more for this symbolic value than for any monetary value – as in the latter sense it is a mere pittance not likely to balance any state budget.

I have begun dispensing these symbolic gifts well in advance of the bicentennial celebration because it will take me from now until that date to cover each of the fifty states. This is much like paying for a birthday gift on a "layaway plan" of advance installments.

Having explained my intentions above, Governor _____, I request and hope that you in your capacity as chief executive of the state of _____ will accept this gift of respect and appreciation on behalf of all the citizens thereof.

I must now confess that in the past I have been harshly critical of certain negative conditions and institutions in America, and I sincerely believed there had been full justification for that critical stance. I was an active and enthusiastic participant in the massive civil rights and anti-war protest demonstrations of the past decade. Many self-proclaimed "patriots" equated such participation with "unAmericanism" and even "treason." Nevertheless, having voluntarily and honorably served America as a naval seaman during World War II, and again having voluntarily made myself available – as an army officer – to serve America in the event of a formal declaration of war stemming from the Korean "police action" – I deeply felt that I had fully earned the indisputable right to protest and criticize that which I knew to be not in the best interest of America's future. Furthermore, patriots – as I interpret patriotism – are not they who seek to keep America that which she now is; or they who seek to return America to that which she once was. The true patriots are they who seek to make America that which she is capable of becoming for the greater glory of God and man.

Today as America approaches her 200th birthday she is shaken and depressed from the recent ignominious fall of a hopelessly-corrupt national administration; she is apprehensively nursing a sick and precariously-tottering national economy; and she is very wearily and painfully searching for an acceptable solution to a volatile racial "school-bussing" issue. Therefore, I now place all criticism of her in abeyance and proceed to praise America for her many inherent virtues as a nation, and express my heartfelt appreciation to her for the many and varied blessings which she has bestowed on me personally – not the least of which was a formal education financed by the World War II "G.I. Bill of Rights."

Even as I caustically criticized America in the past, I was always appreciative of all blessings received and always mindful of the inescapable truth that I am that which I am because America is that which she is – my character having been molded by the American experience and my reaction to that experience. I was always mindful of the fact that my own consciousness is a composite of the con-

sciousnesses of all my fellow Americans of every level of society, from all walks of life, of every color, race, creed, and religion who have in effect keyed their respective knowledge and experiences into the psychic computer banks of my mind. So in truth the people and I are ONE. I and the people are ONE. The people and America are ONE. America and I are ONE. Therefore America's faults are clearly my own faults exteriorized and projected on to the national stage. In criticizing America I merely had been engaging in SELF-CRITICISM.

Her glaring inequities, racial prejudice, gross materialism, and monumental egotism notwithstanding – America has been and still is the mightiest and most honorable among earthly nations, primarily because she is ensouled by a conscientious, generous, and very compassionate people when circumstances clearly require that they express these finer qualities. Considering the extent and complexity of her ethnic mixture and the overwhelming problems involved in administering a nation of her size, it is unfair and unreasonable for anyone to expect her to meet the expectations of every self-interest group which seek and demand satisfaction of one kind or another. It is unreasonable to expect her to be infallible in every decision affecting her foreign and domestic policies. Woefully imperfect as we all are as individuals, and difficult as it is for one person to live in harmony with another, it is sheer folly for anyone to expect a nation – which is but a multiplication and magnification of the individual – to find it any easier to solve infinitely-complex problems of human relations on a massive scale.

Relatively, America is a youthful nation erratically and painfully groping toward an elusive maturity among older nations. She is experiencing her own "generation gap."

Her great strength and redeeming quality lie largely in her amazingly youthful recuperative powers and in her great flexibility – her genius for "rolling with the punches" of fate and effecting change wherever change is clearly desired and required.

Her youthful frailties notwithstanding, America remains the "hope of the world." The ethereal light invisibly beaming from the great copper torch held aloft by the Statue of Liberty still illuminates

71

an ever-darkening world; and still warmly beckons the weary free-dom-loving pilgrim to America's shores. The mighty Liberty Bell still thunderously tones its inducement to the oppressed abroad who are perceptive enough to hear its silent and sacred peal. From the lofty heights of Mt. Rushmore, the gigantic granite visages of Washington, Jefferson, Lincoln, and Roosevelt still focus their eyes out across the American landscape and seem to nod in unanimous agreement that "it is good."

All these sincere, complimentary sentiments aside for the moment—it is of the utmost urgency that America reflects deeply on the present state of her spiritual nature as she prepares to celebrate her birthday. Let her meditate on the words of her national motto: "In God we trust." Let her then ask: "CAN GOD TRUST US?" From her national "Pledge of Allegiance, let America isolate and meditate on this phrase: "...one nation under God..." If she is to continue to receive the divine blessings heretofore so richly and gen-erously bestowed on her by God, it is not enough that America be merely one nation under God – America must be one nation under God and SERVING GOD. It is imperative at this critical junc-ture in time for the American people to make a more determined and concerted effort to see to it that it will be so.

Finally – in gratitude and humility for America citizenship – I say to the United States of America as represented by the great state of _____: 'HAPPY BIRTHDAY' and "Best wishes for many happy birthdays to come.

Most respectfully and very cordially yours,
Thomas Cannon

n 1976 Thomas Cannon got out his old Navy uniform. It was a little tight, but he was able to fit into it. His son, Marshall, took a picture of him posed in front of a large American flag that they had hung across the clothes line to celebrate the Bicentennial. Of course that was not the only way he celebrated the Bicentennial. He sent $50 to the governor of each one of the 50 states and the three territorial possessions along with a letter. He started sending out the letters and checks two years early because it took him a while to accumulate the necessary $2,500. As he sent a letter and postal money order to each governor, he carefully crossed off the state on a large map of the United States.

That was the largest gift he had ever given to any one cause, and it was very well received by the governors of the states. Forty-eight governors responded to his letter, thanking him for his generous donation and the patriotic sentiments he expressed.

Ronald Reagan, then governor of California, wrote in part, "I, too, am grateful for the sentiments you set forth in your inspiring letter. You certainly have taken a unique and positive avenue for expressing your thoughts in regard to our country."

The governor of Virginia, Mills E. Godwin, Jr., wrote, *It is apparent that your comments are heartfelt and you are sincere in recognizing the good that exists while being mindful of the personal commitments that will be needed from our citizens to assure that we as a people and a nation will fulfill the hopes of our founding fathers.*

And Governor George Busbee of Georgia announced Tom's gift at his weekly news conference and praised his generous patriotic gesture. In a letter to Tom he stated, "I accept this gift on behalf of the citizens of Georgia with full appreciation of its symbolic nature as you presented it. I am gratified, as I am sure the governors of other states will be, by the thoughts you expressed in giving this gift."

Sending these monetary gifts to the states probably meant more to Tom than any of the governors could realize. After leaving the Navy, he was discouraged with the system and what he and others called the Jim Crow era. Although he mentioned his participation in civil rights demonstrations in his letter, he did not mention how he felt his government had deceived him when he signed up to serve in the Navy in World War II, and how bitter that made him feel. Shortly after returning to civilian life he felt that our great democracy was all a sham.

But Tom was unique in that he found ways to express his anger that were not only nonviolent, but were also healing for him. He did attend Civil Rights rallies, including the march on Washington where he heard the Reverend Martin Luther King, Jr. give his inspiring "I Have a Dream" speech. Traveling by bus from Richmond to Washington, D.C., he stood in the huge crowd around the Lincoln memorial and listened to the speeches and entertainment provided by folk singers such as Joan Biaz and Peter, Paul and Mary. The day was hot and the sun blazed down on them, but it was an experience he remembers fondly.

While he attended rallies, he did not participate in some of the more violent demonstrations or race riots. Instead, to release the frustration that he felt he drew cartoons, and wrote letters to the editors of local Richmond newspapers. He got the anger out of his system through creative outlets rather than physical ones.

Although the papers would only print a letter from one person every two months, since there were two newspapers in Richmond at that time, he would alternate. One month he would write to the *News Leader*, and then a month later he would fire off a letter to the *Times-Dispatch*.

In one letter to the editor of the *Richmond News Leader*, he defended Malcolm X. Part of his letter stated,

> *"…the purpose of my letter is neither to condemn Malcolm X, nor to assail his essential beliefs. To the contrary – while I firmly disagree with many of his earlier views, especially his all-inclusive condemnation of the white race, I admired him greatly for his dynamic, self-developed-eloquence: his indomitable courage; and his monumental sincerity. I felt I knew how he felt, and knew what he tried to say.*
>
> *Malcolm X believed there was a point of provocation beyond which God, Himself, would*

not expect the Negro to remain "nonviolent," and believed the Negro had passed that point.

Malcolm X believed it was stretching love beyond human endurance and God's tolerance to apply it to that savage, unrepentant breed of white barbarians who dynamite Negro children; who gun down peaceful Negro men; and who burn down Negro churches.

Malcolm X believed the Negro should value God-given life enough to defend it against these barbarous whites and the vile social order which pampers and protects them."

In another letter he criticized the *News Leader's* attacks on Dr. Martin Luther King. On August 12, 1962 his letter appeared in the editorial section. In part he said,

"Your bitter contempt for the Rev. Martin Luther King has been manifested repeatedly in newsprint and on television. Therefore your recent editorial "Of Rights and the Rev. King" (August 10) came not unexpectedly. You label the Rev. King a "typical itinerant professional agitator" and a "psalm singing actor." The Rev. King needs no defense on my part. The worldwide acclaim he has won suffices for his defense, and attests to the rightness of his crusade. However, I do wish to comment on the man and his influence.

In the field of theology, I believe Martin Luther King, Jr. to be the greatest mortal these United States of America have ever produced, or are likely ever to produce. I do further believe him to be the greatest friend your South has ever known, or is ever likely to know. He has dared to teach by example in the field those Christian principles most clergymen dare not even express directly from the safety of the pulpit.

The Rev. King knows there are innumerable Negroes who are hostile toward Jim Crowism, but do not share his philosophy on non-violent resistance. The Rev. King knows these Negroes are seething with justified discontent, merely awaiting the appearance of strong prevalence leadership – as the expanding ranks of Elijah Muhammad's Muslim movement attest. The Rev. King knows each new generation of Negro youth will be less inclined than the previous one to grin and bear the gross indignities imposed on them by the vileness of your cherished Jim Crow traditions."

Tom went on to say, *"Your South would be wise to heed his counsel while there is yet time. His exit from the stage might well be the "cue" for the appearance of the non-pious and non-passive cast of villains waiting impatiently in the wings. Your South had a great friend in*

Abraham Lincoln, but failed to recognize him as such until after his assassination and the advent of "carpetbag" government. Today your South has a great friend in Martin Luther King, Jr., but it is not likely to recognize him as such until his "role" will have been assumed by another "actor" — a non-believer in non-violent demonstrations."

In 1964 he wrote a letter to the editor of the *Times-Dispatch* commenting on an editorial that was labeled "Negroes Disenchanted with Nonviolence." His letter was criticizing an editorial that discussed rioting that had occurred in New York, and compared the racial strife in the North with that occurring in the South.

"...the editor sneeringly compares the current racial strife in the North with that occurring in the South, and as expected he presents the Negro as the arch villain of each locality.

Recent racial strife in New York is not merely a "lesson for the North," it is a lesson for fools at all points of the compass. New York holds no monopoly in this category. The gist of the "lesson" is that an ominously increasing number of Negroes — exclusive of the hoodlum element — no longer subscribes to the philosophy of "non-

violence" under any circumstances and provocations, as taught by the Rev. Martin Luther King."

He ended that letter with this paragraph:

"...this writer certainly does not condone the looting of property and attacks on innocent white citizens by Negro rioters in New York or elsewhere. However, he does share their growing disenchantment with "non-violence" as a defensive measure against a ruthless, treacherous, unrepentant racist enemy to whom deceit, intimidation and violence in his relations with Negroes have always been a way of life."

Not many people could find such suitable ways of expressing their discontent with the racial problems that were such a major part of life in the United States in the 1960's. And ten years after admitting to being disenchanted with "nonviolence" as a means of opposing racial inequalities he was able to state that America remains the "hope of the world" as it approached its Bicentennial anniversary.

This transformation came about largely because he realized that whites were also demonstrating and putting their lives on the line against unfair racial practices. Some young white Civil Rights leaders did lose their lives in an attempt to eliminate racial prejudice from the country and get some of the laws changed. Seeing these sacrifices by whites in an attempt to help correct some of the racial conditions helped Tom change his mind about the future of our country.

Ten years after his Bicentennial tribute he sent a $1,000 check to a campaign launched by the *New York Daily News* to restore the Statue of Liberty. In his letter to Mr. James Wieghart, the editor of the *Daily News* he wrote:

> " *I've had a long-standing, torrid, love affair with New York's grand lady – the Statue of Liberty – even though I've never laid eyes on her.* " He went on to refer to a line from his Bicentennial letter referring to the statue, *"The ethereal light invisibly beaming from the great copper torch held aloft by the Statue of Liberty still illuminates an ever-darkening world; and still warmly beckons the weary, freedom-loving pilgrim to America's shores."*

In 2002 he once again wrote to the governors of each of the United States, the District of Columbia, and the territorial possessions. This time he was responding to the attack on the World Trade Center in 2001, and was not able to send $50 to each state, but sent instead a $1 postal money order to convey the same message of oneness and unity to the nation as he had done for the Bicentennial. He chose July 4th as the date to send this letter because he said that year he felt the nation needed a reminder of its strength and greatness, and was hoping that the symbolic donation would have an uplifting effect during a depressing time. He wrote:

> *"The cohesiveness of and the collective-minded dedication to the preservation of the United States of America and its democratic principles is perhaps more important today than ever before. This is because we now are engaged in an unconventional war with an elusive, shadowy, merciless, fanatical and suicidal Islamic-terrorist enemy. Presumptuously, this enemy has announced publicly his intention to destroy America and Americans. He has punctuated his threat in a most horrifying and devastating manner with his successful September 11, 2001 unprovoked attacks on the World Trade Center in New York City and on the Pentagon in Washington, D.C.*
>
> *On December 7, 1941, another fanatical enemy of America launched a similar successful and unprovoked attack at Pearl Harbor. The U.S. Navy's Pacific Fleet was virtually destroyed. Eventually that audacious enemy reaped the full consequences of his folly many times over. His powerful air force was swept from the Asian sky. His powerful navy was destroyed. His powerful army was driven and crushed from one island to another. His cities*

were fire-bombed into rubble and two of them were incinerated by atomic bombs.

Obviously the Islamic-extremist enemy learned no lesson from the fate of America's World War II enemy. Therefore the former may be destined to be destroyed like the later – perhaps along with those nations that are sponsoring, funding and providing their suicidal Islamic-terrorists proxies with military technology and sanctuary.

In this hour of national peril, I pray for the safety of our beloved nation and encourage all the citizens of your great state to remain steadfast and shoulder-to-shoulder with their fellow citizens of other states; with citizens of our three territorial possessions; with citizens of the District of Columbia; and with our president and Congress.

I wish for you, sir, for your administration, and for all the people of your state a very happy 4th of July holiday celebration – and for many more of them to come.

God Bless America and God bless all the wonderful citizens who ensoul her and make her that which she continues to be – a bright beacon of light, freedom, hope and opportunity for the oppressed and "wretched of the earth" who seek to find a better and more fulfilling way of life.

Very cordially yours,
Thomas Cannon

Chapter 6

Marriage and School

Thomas Cannon at Hampton Institute 1952 (Family Photo)

When Tom went to see Princetta after his return from World War II, he didn't expect her to welcome him with hugs and kisses. They really had just been corresponding as friends, but he did expect a little nicer welcome than the one he got.

She was working as an usher at the Maggie Walker and Booker T. movie theaters on Broad Street in Richmond. He says, "I surprised her and her reaction kind of disappointed me because she turned to a fellow usher, and asked her to get this boy a seat. She acted like I was any member of the public."

Not only was he hurt that she didn't give him a warmer welcome, but to call him a "boy" was an insult. He was a man who had just finished serving his country. Besides that, "boy" was a term used to insult Negroes at that time. As he says, "It seems you went from 'boy' to 'uncle' when you were an old man. Nobody called you a man in those days. But that was from white people who were trying to put you down. I didn't expect that from Princetta."

Tom was living at his brother Joe's, which was not far from where Princetta lived. They began to see each other on a regular basis. They went for walks in the park and to the movies. He often picked her up after work. One night he went to the theater when she wasn't expecting him, and he saw her come out of the theater and walk across the street to the bus stop as if she was going to take the bus home. But when the bus came she didn't get on it, instead she ducked around the corner and met another man who seemed a good bit older than Princetta. Tom was so hurt and disappointed, he thought she'd probably been seeing him all along and that broke his heart. He went to her foster parents and told them about this older man. He was afraid something might happen to her, or she might get pregnant, and they would blame him. When they heard she had been meeting that man after work at the movie theater, they made her quit that job. As he says, "I really had no claim to her – we weren't engaged – but I presumed we'd be serious and get married. I thought after I told her foster parents what was going on she wouldn't have anything to do with me. I guess she forgave me because she continued coming around to see Joe's wife, Nellie, so we worked up a friendship again, and eventually decided to get married."

There was no elaborate ceremony. They went to City Hall to get a license and then one day walked around the block to the house where the pastor of his brother Joe's church lived. The minister's wife and son were at home, so they were the witnesses, and Tom and Princetta were married. It was September of 1946, Friday the 13th.

He says, "She was a beautiful young girl. She had dropped out of school in the ninth grade, so she had more education than I did at that point. She was just seventeen, and she could have done a heck of a lot better than me. Of course, she could have done a lot worse too.

"Our marriage was very simple, no guests, no wedding cake. We couldn't afford a honeymoon, and I didn't even have money for a wedding ring. We were lucky we could afford a place to live. Looking back I often wondered why she married me. I was just a funny looking buck-toothed kid with no future, no money, and no real prospects. I had always been considered a little odd because I was so serious. I had an inquiring mind, and wanted to know the why of everything. Why was this so? Why did people behave like they did? And that turned some people off. So I wasn't popular. I only had half of a seventh grade education. My prospects were not that good. I didn't have anything except my willingness to work hard and to be a good husband.

"This was no love of a lifetime. I think she was more fond of me than in love with me, but I think our marriage must have been predestined even though it was almost like a marriage of convenience or a business partnership. Shortly after we got married I told her, 'You don't love me.' And she said 'Well, I can learn to love you.' Now that was like saying, 'You're right I don't love you.' But she was so young then, she probably didn't know what love was, and I probably didn't either. So this was no great torrid love affair. I think my feelings were deeper than hers were about me, but she was fond of me. At the time she probably wanted a change of environment. But she was basically a good, decent person.

She did what was necessary to be a good housewife and mother, and I did my job as husband. Of course as I realized she didn't have those feelings towards me, my feelings towards her diminished. But we did all right – there was no fussing and fighting.

"She was the ideal wife for me. She was brought up in poverty herself, so she didn't expect fancy cars or jewelry or anything. And she was tolerant enough to let me live my life as I saw fit, and I treasured her for that. She was ideally suited with me to begin my philanthropic mission when that time came. There were good years and some bad times. Still, our marriage lasted for 54 years, and we raised two sons. So for the most part it was a good marriage, and it proves you don't need a big flashy, expensive wedding to make a marriage work."

Before her marriage, Princetta had led a hard life. She was abandoned by her mother and raised by the midwife that delivered her. That family had another foster daughter, and at one time she told Princetta that her real mother had tried to kill her shortly after she was born. Although it didn't say so on her birth certificate, her father must have been white because she was very fair. She looked more Indian than black with her long straight hair. Her appearance made her stand out from her schoolmates who picked on her for looking so different. She looked different from her foster parents too because they were dark. She suffered because of her color. There was prejudice all around then – whites who didn't like blacks, blacks who didn't like whites, and even some blacks who didn't like blacks that had lighter skin tones. But Princetta embraced everyone; color didn't matter to her. Her foster parents had one grandson who was mentally retarded, and another one who made her feel uncomfortable because he tried to proposition her. She wanted to get out of that situation and have a place of her own.

Fortunately Tom heard about a man who wanted to get rid of his apartment and furniture because his marriage was breaking up. Tom had a couple of hundred dollars that he had saved from his naval pay, and that was just enough to pay for that apartment. So Tom and Princetta didn't have to buy any furniture. It was in a rundown, rat-infested part of town, but it was all they could afford.

Rats were nothing new to Tom as there had been rats in the area where his brother Joe lived. He remembered one night when he was staying with them and they heard a terrific screeching coming from downstairs. Joe had bought a chicken to kill and eat, and it was in a crate on a table in the kitchen. When they went into the kitchen they saw the poor thing in a horrible state. The chicken had a hole in its back where a rat had attacked it. The rat had been trying to eat it alive.

Tom said the city used to put poison out in the alleys to try to kill the rats, but they stopped doing that either because they ran out of money or it was dangerous to have that poison around with children in the area. He set his own traps out, and he eventually got a .22 rifle and used to stand out on the porch at night and shoot the ones he could see.

Rats weren't the only problem in that neighborhood. There were some unsavory characters, too. Their apartment was on the ground floor, and the elderly man who lived in the apartment above them warned Tom about one of those men. He told Tom to be careful because this man made moonshine and at night would come to their backyard and hide his "shine" in a hole he had dug there. A neighbor told him to get his moonshine out of there because they would be the ones that got in trouble if the police found it there. Of course that was the whole idea, he knew better than to hide it around his place because the police were probably watching him.

After a year Thomas, Jr. was born, and money became even tighter. Princetta got a job in a laundry as a clothes sorter, and a lady kept the baby while she worked. Tom took whatever work he could find. He worked for a brick contractor and did construction work, and he worked at a textile mill. Tom soon realized that to get a better job and be able to support a family, he would have to go back to school and finish his high school education.

He says, "I decided to go back to high school for the same reason most people go to college, to be able to support my family better. I wanted to go and develop my mind, and be qualified for a better job with a better salary. I thought I could get a job with the post office which would pay better than anything else I could get, but you needed a high school diploma to qualify for that."

He enrolled at Maggie Walker High School after being out of school for almost ten years. There were other veterans in his classes doing the same thing, so he didn't feel out of place among all the young students. And the classes were a snap for him.

"Even though my schooling had been interrupted I still kept reading and growing. I read everything I could get my hands on – newspapers, magazines, books – whatever interested me. I kind of gave myself almost the equivalent of a high school education through all the reading that I did. I didn't stop growing because I dropped out of school. I was still inquisitive and tried to learn everything I could from whatever source was available."

But he was just sliding by, even sleeping through some of his classes because he was working all night at the textile mill.

Like many other Maggie Walker students he rode the Richmond Transit System bus to school. One day some of the black students on the bus began shouting insults out the window to some white people they were passing on the street. Tom was concerned for two reasons: one, he didn't want the school to get a bad name because of the action of those few students and two, he was afraid if that kind of behavior continued it might start a race riot. So he wrote a letter to the student government telling them what happened, and explaining his concern. Somehow a teacher got hold of the letter and instead of letting the students handle the matter themselves, which was what Tom hoped would happen, she took the letter to the *Richmond Afro-American*, a black newspaper that was published at that time. A reporter made a big deal out of the letter, and wrote an article about how things were out of hand at Maggie Walker; so naturally everyone was mad at Tom. The students, teachers and administrators weren't mad at the teacher who took the letter and took it to the newspaper, they were mad at him.

When it was time for Princetta to give birth to their second child, Tom went to the assistant principal and asked if he could be excused for half that day because his wife was having a baby. She turned him down. He felt she had something against veterans because she said something like, "You veterans, you always want special treatment. No, you can't go." He said he told her, "Well, I was just being polite asking if I could go, but I'm going anyway." Fortunately the principal learned about the problem, and he got approval to leave school for that half day to be with Princetta when their second son, Calvin Marshall, was born.

Finally one of his eighth-grade teachers, Mrs.

Beatrice Cox, and the school guidance counselor, Mrs. Kate Henderson, realized that the high school material wasn't challenging enough for him, and told him that he could probably qualify for college and use the GI Bill to pay for that education. He never dreamed of entering college, but they convinced him to take the necessary tests to qualify. As he says, "They literally kicked me out of high school and into college, and I'm forever grateful to them for that."

He enrolled at Hampton Institute and chose art education as his major and English as his minor. He didn't really want to be an art teacher, but he enjoyed drawing - especially cartoons - and he knew that he would be able to get a good paying job as an art teacher.

He wanted to bring Princetta and his two boys down to Hampton, and get an apartment and live off campus, but he didn't have enough money to do that. Instead his mother came from Chase City and stayed with Princetta while he was in school, and he paid her a little stipend to compensate her.

He says, "College wasn't a happy time for me. I really didn't belong, and I never fit in. I never thought I'd ever set foot on a college campus. I was just aiming to get a high school diploma when I went back to school, and I really wasn't prepared for college. I certainly wasn't prepared for the institution of hazing. I didn't know anything about it. I had never heard of it. So when I joined the freshman class and they put this little green beanie on my head and a nametag around my neck with a green ribbon, it annoyed me. That was kid's stuff. This hazing was done by these kids fresh out of high school, and I considered myself a war veteran and a family man. I didn't feel like I had to take any guff off these little kids that just left their mamma's apron strings.

"Hampton's colors are blue and white. I was wearing a black sweater with the red letter "C" on my pocket, and the upper classmen didn't like that. I think those were Davidson College's colors, but I just liked red and black, that's why I was wearing it. I knew what Hampton's colors were. But some of the big football players approached me in the cafeteria and accosted me. They said, 'Freshman, what are Hampton's colors?' I said, 'Blue and white.' They said, 'Yeah, but you're wearing black and red.' I told them I liked black and red, and they didn't do anything in the cafeteria, but afterwards a mob of students, it looked like it was about 20 or more, they grabbed me and dragged me up in this foyer – I guess so the dean couldn't see what was going on. One of them slapped me on the side of the head. It didn't hurt anything but my pride, but then they took a razor blade and cut my red "C" off my sweater. I was furious – absolutely furious. I wasn't scared of them, and when they let me go I went straight to the Dean of Men's home and told him what happened. I also wrote him a fiery letter about the indignation I felt about the treatment I was receiving because I didn't know about any college hazing. If I had had four years of high school, I would have known what to expect, but I kind of leap-frogged over high school, and didn't know that hazing was all in fun. After I sounded off on the Dean of Men, I didn't have any more problems. I can laugh at it now, but it wasn't funny then because I went there to get an education. I wasn't going there for foolishness. I felt I'd outgrown all that kid stuff. I didn't see why I had to wear that stupid green beanie, and a dog tag around my neck. So that was the first conflict I had on the campus."

Eventually he became kind of popular because he started drawing cartoons about the football team. They were poster-sized, and there was a line of bulletin boards that were glass-encased, and he put them up there. He usually made one before the football game and one after. The football team was the Hampton Pirates because the campus was on the waterfront. The mascot was a pirate, and if they went to a college in North Carolina to play a game and lost, he would draw a cartoon of the Pirates with their seats torn out running up the highway with a sign pointing to Hampton, and the other team's mascot chasing them. If they won he might show them in a victory parade being carried on the shoulders of the students. The kids on campus seemed to enjoy them, and each time he put one up it would draw a crowd of onlookers. He says, "I got a big kick out of doing those posters, but the time I spent drawing them I probably should have been studying."

His fellow students might have enjoyed the cartoons, but the head of the art department didn't. He had been an internationally renown portrait painter, and he was very serious about art and didn't want any of his students fooling around with cartoons.

Tom says, " He was Austrian and claimed he went to art school with Adolph Hitler. He took art very seriously. I guess he thought I was corrupting art with my cartoons. But we were not all there to become artists. Most of us were training to become art teachers, and the emphasis should have been on crafts that we could share with our young students. To be a good art teacher in the elementary schools the emphasis needs to be on crafts – things students can make out of paper and wood and clay – not oil painting and stuff like that; but our teacher was focused on fine arts, and the program wasn't set up to turn out fine artists, but art teachers. And what wasn't fine arts was on the philosophy of teaching, and I hated that. Oh, my goodness how I hated that!

"I wanted to spend more time painting and drawing and making ceramics. I wanted to try to master what I was going to teach. I couldn't see myself being an art teacher and not knowing how to create art – but the emphasis was all on the academic side of art teaching, so that's where my professors and I had a conflict. A lot of us had to use our own time to get into the studio and work with different art materials.

"During your freshman year you were required to

live on campus, so I lived in a men's dormitory – James Hall. The first year was great because I was eating in the cafeteria. But the second year I moved off campus to save money, and I didn't have those cafeteria coupons anymore. Those were some tough years because I was often hungry, and I missed my family. I was scraping rock bottom because I was sending money home to Princetta to pay for food and bills, so that didn't leave much for me. My mother was staying with Princetta at the time, and I paid her $15 a month while I was at Hampton. It wasn't much, but it was a heck of a lot of money to me at that time. Sometimes it was torture to walk across campus at dinnertime and smell the food coming from the cafeteria. My supper usually came from a vending machine, and was Nabs and NuGrape. I didn't starve, but it was rough."

The one bright spot during that time was his friendship with Benjamin Wigfall. They were not room-mates, but they were living in the same house off-campus. Ben lived downstairs and Tom lived upstairs, and they spent a lot of time together. Ben was the type of talented, serious artist their professor enjoyed teaching. He went on to get an advanced degree in art at the State University of Iowa. On a visit to Hampton he was invited to teach art there, which he did for several years. Then he moved to New York and taught at the State University of New York at New Paltz. He also set up a community organization called Communications

Village and opened an art gallery – the Watermark/ Cargo Gallery in Kingston, New York. Wigfall has the distinction of being the first, and youngest, black artist to have a painting purchased by the Virginia Museum of Fine Arts. It was selected when he was a sophomore at Hampton.

Like Tom, Ben had never thought he would go to college. He says, "I never dreamed about going to college. I thought it was something other people did. But in English class at Armstrong High School we discussed a quote, and I think it was from Emerson, and the quote was "insist on yourself." The teacher explained that it meant you must rely on yourself, you must listen to yourself and rely on your judgment. That was one of the things that made me decide to follow my art interest."

Wigfall got several scholarships that enabled him to attend Hampton. But he says that he was basically naïve when he went to college. "I really thought that when I got on the campus I would hear college songs and see people into deep study on the lawn. I had one of these crazy romantic pictures. I thought everybody would be in deep study. When I first got there I went to the library and was overwhelmed, not only because I finally got to reach college, but because I saw all those books and I felt like I had to read every one of them. I assigned myself that task, and I only had four years to do it, so that was a pretty overwhelming task.

"Tom and I got along well. We agreed basically on

most things. We never had any hassles, but we did have true, real arguments. We would take opposing points of view and put them up against each other and see which worked best. I think he was always trying to find something – what his purpose was or what his reason for being here was. He was a very thorough person. We were never afraid to tackle a job, either on the physical or mental level. Whatever it took to get the thing done. I appreciated him for that – he didn't take any shortcuts. He was a very honest person. Not just that he wouldn't steal something, but he was straightforward and consistent with what he believed."

Ben and Tom liked to have fun, too. Ben taught Tom how to play chess and a card game called Tonk. Some nights instead of studying they stayed up late talking about the meaning of life or playing cards or chess. They were both in the same economic straits, what Wigfall now calls their "starving times," and he remembers that sometimes their food supply got so low that they played cards for the last orange.

Looking back Tom says, "Ben and I used to talk about deep things like the meaning of life. We fed off each other. I learned from him and he learned from me, and we had a good time in the process."

Even his friendship with Ben could not keep him from missing his wife and boys. He tried to visit them when he could, but he didn't have bus fare to

Richmond, so as he says, "I got out on the highway and rode my thumb. I had to hitchhike to Richmond and hitchhike back to Hampton. That was relatively easy back then, and I had a good little gimmick that I used. I used to earn a little extra money painting a pirate, Hampton's mascot, on the back of students' jackets using textile paints. So I had my own jacket with a painting of the Hampton pirate with a skull and crossbones on his hat. I would get on the side of the highway and I'd be limping along like I could barely make it. Eventually some motorist would come along and feel sorry for me because I looked like I was on my last legs. They'd see that Hampton Institute over the top of the pirate so they knew I was a student, and they'd give me a ride."

But Princetta and his mother weren't getting along, and at one point he said he was going to quit college. His mother said, "You can't quit yet. I haven't saved up enough money." Like many who were poor she felt that money would solve all her problems, and she wasn't about to give up that money that he was paying her. Naturally he was upset because his mother was more concerned about losing that little bit of money that she was getting than she was about him not completing his education. Princetta and his mother finally said they could tolerate each other long enough for him to finish school, but knowing that they were having problems weighed on his mind.

Princetta wasn't a good letter writer either, so Tom

often went to the mailbox only to find it empty. That added to his stress. As he says, "You can't study when you're worrying about all these things. Once I painted a picture of a screaming, detached head because that was the type of emotion I was feeling and going through at that time. But I got all that emotion out of my system and into that painting. I called it *Crescendo*. It was a release of tension and frustration. If I had kept all that bottled up in me, I might have blown up myself!"

The greatest lesson he learned at Hampton came not from any of his professors or anyone on the faculty, but from a visiting entertainer. And he didn't fully understand the lesson until years after he left Hampton.

Marion Anderson, the opera singer, was performing at Hampton, and Tom was in the audience with the rest of the students and faculty members enjoying her singing immensely. Then he noticed that before each song she sang she said, "We will sing this for you." or "Now we're going to sing this song." Tom thought, "What's that woman talking about. I don't see anybody on that stage signing but her. Why does she keep saying 'we'? I looked at the pianist and didn't see his lips moving. He wasn't a ventriloquist. But she acted as if she had a choir with her. I didn't find out what she meant until years after I left Hampton and got her autobiography, *My Lord What a Morning* and read it. She was attributing this 'we' she said before every song to the people who had helped her become what she was. She was including her music teacher, her friends and family. So in essence she was giving them credit and saying they were helping her sing each time she performed a song.

"I thought about that and remembered hearing people talk about somebody being a self-made man. There is no such thing. All of us are the product of the guidance, love, and understanding of a number of people who made us what we are. We are a composite of all the different people we come in contact with and gain wisdom and knowledge from. You can't possibly be a self-made man. We come into this world knowing nothing, and people teach us how to walk, talk, and read. They are building us, and we are a reflection of their love, caring and guidance. Each person is a composite of other people, and when you realize this you can't help but be accepting of other people from other races and other walks of life. When you reach that level of understanding, you see the whole. You don't segment it – it's the cosmic whole which each of us is a part of. Dr. Albert Schweitzer talked about this when he talked about reverence for life – all forms of life."

Another lesson he learned at Hampton came from his ceramics teacher, Joseph Gilliard, who said that his art was as great at that created by Michelangelo or Da Vinci. Tom couldn't understand what he was saying, but eventually came to understand that he meant that each of us is what he or she is intended to be, and he excelled in pottery. Michelangelo couldn't create pottery like he did, and he couldn't paint like Michelangelo, but he wasn't supposed to. He made a big impression on Tom with that statement because as he says, "He made me understand that each of us has a role to play in life, and no one else can be substituted for us."

Tom carried that over into his philanthropy in later years by trying to encourage people to have faith and to believe in themselves. He says that was the hardest thing that black people had to deal with during the Jim Crow era and under segregation. They were made to feel inferior, and it was difficult for many not to succumb to that.

When it came time for Tom's class to graduate, he found out that he had a deficiency in English literature which was a course in his minor. He says, "To succeed you must not only know the work, but put down the information in time on tests, and I had trouble doing that. I'm very slow in everything I do. I read slowly, I write slowly. I guess I had a different speed governor put in me at birth, and that has handicapped me to a certain extent. One of my teachers told me I would be handicapped because I was slow, and she was right. You can know the book from cover to cover, but if you can't get a certain amount of material down in a specified time you flunk. So that's the way I was. When I got that deficiency, I probably knew that boring material, but I didn't put enough of it down in time to get a passing grade on the final. The professor told me she was sorry, but she didn't make the rules and couldn't let me graduate. I was going to leave Hampton and never come back because I was so disgusted that one course could keep me from graduating.

Fortunately, Dr. Stephen Wright, the Dean of Faculty, and Dr. Hugh Gloster, the Chairman of the Communication Center (which English came under) talked to him, and told him he had enough left on his GI bill that he could go to summer school and make up those credits and still graduate. So he went to Virginia Union University the summer of 1953 and took two courses. He did well in both of them and graduated from Hampton with the class of 1954.

He was hoping Princetta would want to go back to school too and get her high school diploma, but she didn't have the desire to develop her mind. He says, "She and I were radically different when it came to academics. She didn't have the desire to read, study, or learn new things. I never tried to force any of it on her. I just let her be herself, and I guess that's why we got along all those years. But I often feared that she would go through the terrible experience that my mother did when my father died if she didn't have a better education. She wasn't fortunate enough to come up in a home like I did where reading was a part of life."

As soon as he graduated from Hampton he had a job teaching art in the Richmond Public Schools as an elementary art consultant. He didn't really think he would like teaching, but it was a bread-and-butter decision. He knew he had to get a job that could support his family and teaching offered that opportunity. He soon found out that he didn't fit in as a teacher. He found it a frustrating job and didn't feel that he could accomplish anything. He taught at Carver Elementary School and the old Buchanan school. As an elementary consultant he was supposed to work with every teacher in each school. At Carver he had 44 teachers, so he'd start an activity with the students, but by the time he'd go to the other 43 teachers it was almost six weeks before he could get back to that class, and they had lost interest in the project by then.

After the first year he wanted to quit, but his supervisor, Miss Helen Rose, talked him into giving it one more year, and she gave him a high school class at Armstrong. But he still had two elementary schools, plus three hours at Armstrong. During the second year Miss Rose told him he wasn't fitting in socially with the other teachers. He thought, "What time did I have to fraternize with the other teachers with two elementary schools and a high school? Besides, I wasn't in teaching for a popularity contest, I was there to teach the children. I loved the children, but I didn't like the system, so I finally quit."

During this time he and Princetta looked for a new house. They found one they liked near Maymont Park which would have been wonderful for them and the two boys, but he needed $500 for a down payment and he only had $250. While he was trying to come up with the rest of the money for the down payment on that house, someone else came along with $500 and bought it. So they purchased a house in the East End on 22nd Street. They were back in a rat-infested neighborhood and could hear them scurrying around in the walls. By this time his attitude towards rats and mice had changed, either from reading Dr. Albert Schweitzer's views on reverence towards all life or reading other writers and simply maturing. He told Princetta, "As long as they stay on their side of the wall, I'm not going to bother them." And he didn't. He also thought back to the birds he had killed when he was a young boy and felt badly, even though he had just been doing what all country boys and the men were doing – hunting game.

He decided to build a birdhouse in his backyard, and he built a very elaborate one. As his little jab at the Jim Crow system, he put a sign on the roof that said "Sky High Café – No blackbirds allowed."

Not only did the birds come to his yard, but other animals did too – a little dog they adopted and named Chico, a cat that had kittens in a tire in the backyard and a neighbor's dog named Prince. Tom always had a soft spot in his heart for animals, and that was eventually reflected in some of his philanthropic gifts.

Chapter 7

Officer Raysa

October 25, 2002

Dear Mr. Boone,

Today I read the "Personality" column in the Richmond Free Press *featuring Officer Mark D. Castillo of the Richmond Bureau of Police. I salute Officer Castillo for his having won the Sherwood Reeder Award for being the City's outstanding employee for 2002.*

I am equally impressed by the great love and respect Officer Castillo expresses for his canine partner and "fellow officer," Raysa.

Officer Castillo credited Raysa for having helped him to win the Sherwood Reeder Award and the $1,000 check that came with it. As an equal member of their team, "Officer Raysa" also deserves full recognition and reward for her devotion to duty and for her years of faithful police work.

Therefore I am matching the $1,000 check given to Officer Mark Castillo with the enclosed one for his dog. After all, it was "Officer Raysa" who has had to poke her nose into all the hot spots while sniffing around for hidden bombs.

Please have one of your staff members deliver my check to Officer Castillo for Raysa. Tell him to use the money for her needs and pleasure.

Also tell him to have his wife cook a big, thick, juicy steak as a special treat for Raysa – and tell Mrs. Castillo to "hold the onions."

Thanks a lot and best wishes always!

Cordially yours,
Tom Cannon

Most of us don't give a second thought to something as ordinary as a white terrycloth towel. To Officer Mark Castillo it is a training tool, and to his dog Raysa - a member of the Richmond Canine Unit - it is her favorite toy.

Officer Castillo says, "We go through thousands of towels. We train the scent dogs by putting a towel in a box with whatever it is we want them to learn to find. You have to isolate that odor and make sure you don't have any contaminants. There can't be two or three things. You have to make sure you have the odor you want them to find, and then you just introduce it to them. If we want them to find dynamite we put the towel in a suitcase full of dynamite, and it picks up that scent. Then we hide the towel, and when the dog finds it they get to play with it. We do that over and over, and the odor gets associated with play. Then you move on, and it gets a little more technical as you go, but basically you do that over and over and over with each odor you want them to learn. Basic training takes about 13 weeks. When they're working and find what they are looking for, they get to play as a reward."

At one time most canine units depended on donated dogs, but unfortunately only about one out of 80 donated dogs turned out to be suited for police work. Now most departments buy dogs, and it has gotten a little expensive. They buy dogs from vendors who import the dogs from overseas. They have already tested the dogs to be police dogs, and to do the things that the police departments are looking for. As Castillo says, "We might spend $2,000 to $3,000 for a dog, but it's guaranteed to work. So if it doesn't work out - for whatever reason - then you can send it back, and they will send you a replacement. The dogs have undergone initial testing to make sure they have the drive and willingness to do the work that we're looking for. They're usually a year-and-a-half to three years old. Most of the dogs are German Sheperds, Dutch Sheperds or Malinois - a Belgian breed. They're all about the size of a German Sheperd or a little smaller. These dogs can work longer than some other breeds. I generally work my dog 20 minutes, and then let her take a break. Dogs are trained for specific work. Raysa is trained to find explosives, whether it's a bomb, gun or ammunition. Some do article searches. If someone robs a bank and they run through the woods and drop the money, the dog can find the money. Other dogs are tracking dogs. If someone runs from the police, and you know where they started from, the dog can pick up ground disturbance and find the person. Others are trained to find missing persons, and some are trained to find narcotics."

Officer Castillo started working with Raysa in 1997. She is a Dutch Sheperd, and he describes her as a "funny-looking German Sheperd." The breed comes in a brindle pattern, kind of tiger-striped. They can be either light with dark stripes or dark with lighter brindling. Raysa is dark. He says, "Everybody has his own dog. No matter whether you're working utility or narcotics or explosives. You're certified as a team. Nobody else works my dog, and I don't work anybody else's dog. The dog goes home with you. That's one of the requirements for a canine officer – that you have a house where you can keep a dog. So the dog goes home with you every day. The only time you don't have the dog might be if you go on vacation and are going to be out of town. Then you can take it to the canine unit where we have kennels, and other people in the unit will take care of your dog. But other than that they're with you."

New people to the canine squad are told that these are work animals, and you're not supposed to treat them like a pet. But, as he says, "That's kind of hard because you're with them every day, basically 24 hours. And you take care of them at work, at home and even on your days off. So you do get very attached to them. I don't care what anybody says, you do get attached to your dog. You do treat them somewhat like a pet, but you have to have some limitations especially for the detective dogs who work narcotics and explosives because their reward for working is play. So if you play with them too much when they're not working then they probably think, "Well, I don't really have to work if I get to play all the other times."

Castillo was told he won the Sherwood Reeder Award as city employee of the year because of the work he did after the attack on the World Trade Center and the Pentagon on September 11, 2001.

"Basically after 9/11 everything went crazy. Since we're the only ones on the Richmond force that work the bomb threats we were called out every day. I don't remember how many calls we had. I had to come back from vacation and work on my days off. It was just a constant thing, and some of those calls take two or three hours to take care of. I've got my son, and sometimes I had to get someone to watch him. One reason it was so hectic is that we don't just respond to things in the city, we respond throughout the state of Virginia. Anybody that needs assistance – they call and we go. So we're not just on call for the city of Richmond. We go to Chesterfield County, Hanover County, Buckingham County, Mecklenburg County. Some of these places are two or three hours away. Sometimes the locations are too big for just one person and one dog to handle, like a large department store. If it's a large building you have to get someone to help you because you'd be there for days if you tried to handle it yourself. But all the canine units are unique in that no matter what department you're from, we work real closely together. So, we're always helping each other. Sometimes we have to call the State Police to assist us," Castillo says.

They haven't found any actual bombs this year. They've found guns and ammunition and things like that from crime scenes. However, they never know when they go out on a call if this might be the time the bomb is real. The dog is not put in any more danger than necessary. If they know a bomb is present, then the bomb squad takes care of it. Castillo is also a bomb technician for the city. He says, "If something is already found, the dog is not used. We've had a few real devices, but we get a lot of hoax devices. When you have people make things up to look like a bomb, you have to treat it like a bomb - especially after 9/11. We get a lot of suspicious packages, or something that a person thinks is a bomb for whatever reason. So basically if someone else thinks it's a bomb, we think it's a bomb until we're 100% sure it's not.

"When I was given the award I told them the only reason I got the award was because of Raysa. She basically does all the work. I'm with her, but if I didn't have her and she wasn't such a good dog, we wouldn't be able to do what we do."

He and his family were shocked when Mr. Cannon gave them the check for Raysa. He says he thought it was extremely generous of him, and it was very nice to be able to buy things for her that he could never do before. The city pays for her food, but he must provide anything else. He says, "I talked to him personally and thanked him, and he was really adamant that all the money went to the dog. I got her an extremely nice doghouse that I would never have been able to afford without his check. I bought things for her that I couldn't get through the city like special leashes, toys, and bags of treats. Every penny of it went to Raysa."

Tom gave the $1,000 gift to Raysa, who he calls "Officer Raysa," because he says, "We humans need to give more respect to animals. They are life forms just as we are, and have been created by the same Creator as we have. They are living, feeling life forms. By giving a $1,000 check to Raysa, I was trying to give her due recognition."

Police Chief Andre Parker also feels that the work of the canine teams is very important to the work the police do in the city of Richmond. Parker says, "On frequent occasions we have opportunities to deal with some of the most dangerous and difficult people and circumstances, and our canine units are part of our team. The dog and handler do a variety of things, one of which is to detect explosives. In this post 9/11 era where we are confronted with the possibility of terrorism on a daily basis it is important that our officers are well-trained, our canine teams are well-trained, and that they are able to detect anything that might be harmful to our residents. So the work that they do is important and also very dangerous. The dogs go into circumstances and situations where we would not send our officers into until we've gotten some sort of indication that it's safe to do so. Because of the unique capabilities that our dogs have they can detect explosive materials in sometimes difficult circumstances. They also track guns that have been used in violent crimes. Frequently the criminal will commit a shooting and flee from the scene. As he flees, he disposes of the weapon, and we need that weapon as a part of our evidentiary presentation during our investigation and subsequent prosecution. So our dogs really do a fantastic job. They also provide an additional partner for the officer. They can see and hear things when the officer is on the street. Our dogs are separated into those that handle explosives, those that track, and dogs that are patrol dogs, that are used to assist the officer in crowd control or individual safety and building searches.

"Can you imagine going into a darkened building at 3:00 a.m. when you have no idea what's going on? You can't see, can't hear, you think behind every door, around every corner there could be a person with a gun. Well, our dogs have the capability of alerting and making sure that our people are aware of the presence of these types of people, or any persons for that matter. They also help us when we have people who have been lost or injured or are disoriented - for example when there's an Alzheimer's patient that walks away from a home. Often that person is disoriented and has no idea where he or she might be going or what the conditions are, and the families are brokenhearted. They don't know what's happened to them, so we use our dogs to track them if we have a good scent. At the same time if we have a suspect in a crime that we need to apprehend, we use our dogs for that as well. So they play a very valuable role in what we do in our everyday work here in the police department."

Sometimes the dogs don't find what they are looking for, and that is hard for the team to accept, but sometimes that does happen. Just as he has to reinforce and encourage his officers when they're out there doing such difficult work, the same thing is important for the dogs. They need encouragement and reinforcement as well. But according to Chief Parker, "The dogs get rewards. They get little treats. The officers don't get little treats, they get a pat on the back, a hearty handshake, and a 'thank you' from the chief."

Tom has always been a big supporter of the police. He feels that they are often underpaid and under appreciated, and that they get criticized for doing the very job that they are hired to do.

In 1979 he composed a poem called *Who Cries for the Cop* because he felt that people were taking the police for granted and didn't really care about them. Unfortunately two days after he wrote the poem Richmond policeman Michael P. Connors was killed in the line of duty, so the poem was dedicated to him as well as to the men and women of the Richmond Police Department. The Fraternal Order of Police Ladies Auxiliary used that poem in a half-page ad in the *Richmond Times-Dispatch*, requesting that people write then Richmond Mayor Henry Marsh to express their concern for the police and let him know that the lack of support for the police created a situation that was at a critical point.

The title of that poem along with his drawing of a police officer and the words "Support our Police" was also repeated on several billboards that he paid for and had placed around the city of Richmond. One was on top of a building on Broad Street, another on Adams Street, and another was at the corner of 4th and Franklin Streets. By coincidence someone else had purchased a billboard next to one of his that said, "Warning – You are in Richmond. Our police are undermanned, underpaid, and under-equipped. Use extreme caution while here!" Many people thought he paid for that billboard too, but he had nothing to do with it – although he agreed with what it said.

Tom has made several other gifts to police officers or their families. One went to the top graduate of Richmond's 43rd Basic Police School, Lloyd E. Redford, in 1980. Although he told then-police-chief Frank S. Duling that the check was earned by academic excellence, in his letter to Duling he added, *Hopefully, this gift will help toward boosting the morale of Patrolman Redford and his fellow officers throughout the department and assure them that they are much appreciated both as vital servants of our society and just fine human beings.*

Lt. Charles W. Bennett, Jr., then Officer-In-Charge of the Training Division responded to Cannon's gift with a letter stating, "This act will certainly help raise the morale of the Bureau, which is greatly needed in these troubled times. I want you to know that we in the Police Training Division look upon you as one of our special friends, and that we cherish that friendship."

Bumper stickers Tom designed and had printed saying "Support our Police," lapel buttons, a series of inspirational tapes he purchased for the Richmond Police Department, and two gifts to police officers' widows are just some of the other ways he has used his monetary gifts to show his appreciation for the work police officers do. The widow of one police officer wrote him and explained that useful as the money was to her, the message of encouragement he sent in the letter he wrote to her was more important. He says, "That made me feel real good because that's what the giving is about. The money is really a symbol of caring and concern. Nobody is going to get rich from $1,000. The money is useful, but the more important thing is that somebody thinks so much of you that they give you a gift."

He says, "Years ago I noticed there were almost no public voices to be heard speaking out on behalf of our often-beleaguered police officers throughout our nation. Relatively few citizens dared to speak out publicly to defend them against their frequently harsh and often unfair critics. Therefore I decided to take upon myself the task of defending them and championing their cause openly and publicly. Our police officers rep-

resent the last line of defense between a civilized society and the savagery of the jungle. They need, and should
receive, all the love, support and encouragement they
can get from the public for the highly dangerous and
stressful job they are hired to perform on a daily basis.

"We hire them to enforce the law, and paradoxical-
ly, citizens often criticize them for trying to do so. We
complain about a high crime rate, and then criticize the
police for laying hands on the culprits who are commit-
ting the crimes. Sometimes it looks like people have
more sympathy for the criminals than for the people
who are trying to protect us from them. Citizens are
quick to shout "police brutality," but significantly they
don't offer a sympathetic word of concern when a criminal brutalizes or even kills a police officer. This is why
I composed my poem, *Who Cries for the Cop?*

"I think police officers are the most underpaid,
under-supported and over-criticized public servants in
the nation. Considering this reality, I often wonder why
any man or woman would ever want to consider pursu-
ing a career in law enforcement. Obviously, these wonderful and courageous people who choose this profes-
sion know the vital importance of police work and have
a much stronger devotion to public service than I have.
They know their community needs to be, and must be,
protected at all costs.

"The public must be reminded that our police officers are family people like the rest of us. They have chil-

dren to raise and educate just like other parents. That's why I have made gifts to the families of officers killed on the job and recently to Hanover County sheriff's investigator Tommy Eaves. Eaves was infected with acute hepatitis C after arresting a burglary suspect. The suspect put up a fight in an area with thorny bushes, and both the suspect and Eaves were cut by the thorns. The suspect admitted to using drugs and had contracted hepatitis, which was passed on to Eaves."

Tom also stated that by giving his monetary gift to Eaves he hoped to raise the public consciousness of the dangers our police officers are exposed to on a daily basis. He says, "My gift to Tommy Eaves was one of the most satisfying to me because of the impact it had on him. I met him at the Peace Officer's Memorial Breakfast, and he said until he received my check he had been very bitter about his problems. He was feeling that fate was unfair, and that he felt like the world had turned against him by giving him another disease to fight. That was the mood he was in. He'd already battled cancer, his child had had cancer, and then he contracted hepatitis arresting a criminal. There seemed to be no relief to his problems. The way he explained it to me, my gift and letter lifted him out of his depression. Since it had already given him what it needed to do, he gave the money away to cancer research."

In a letter to Tom, Mrs. Eaves said that his check and inspirational letter arrived at a time when they were feeling down and needed the lift that his support brought. She wrote, "You've done more for us than you'll probably ever know. Thank you from the bottom of our hearts."

Chief Parker also appreciates Tom's support. He says, "Shortly after I arrived here in Richmond, I learned of Tom Cannon's generosity and some of the things he had done. I had the pleasure of meeting him and speaking with him, and I was very impressed with his open heart and desire to help. I was not aware that he was not a wealthy man. I was surprised to find that he is a man of working class just like all of us, and has done the best that he could with what he had. I was very impressed with the fact that giving money away through his philanthropy is not the same as a person with wealth and concurrent social status making philanthropic gifts. So I was very surprised by that, and I was very humbled by that. He is genuinely a wonderful man.

"His support of the police is very important to our department. I hate to use the analogy of the encouragement and support that we give to our canine teams, but it's the same thing for a human being. From early childhood development we all know that we operate better, more efficiently, and more socially when we have support and reinforcement; whether it is from a family member or from someone else. The support that he gives to the police department is very important to their morale. It's good to have a voice out there that is supportive of the work we do and not critical of everything that we do. I'm so very proud of all or our officers. They do a very difficult and dangerous job every day for the welfare of this community and they often feel that the community does not support them. The fact that they could lose their life doing that work is not given the gravity that it should be.

"Just recently another police officer was killed doing his job. This has been a horrible 18 months for the law-enforcement community in the Commonwealth of Virginia. More officers were killed in these last 18 months than ever in the history of the state. It is sad to see that. You see these fresh-faced young men and women who are very idealistic when they start this job, and then over a period of time they get worn down. The environment they work in grinds them down, and when there is no support from the public it really wears them down. It's hard for me as chief to keep their morale up and to keep their spirits up, and I work very hard to do that. So when we have members from the community like Mr. Cannon who are coming forward and making an extraordinary effort to recognize our officers, and to tell us how appreciative he is of the work we do it really makes us feel good, and I know our officers would all say the very same thing."

Chief Parker went on to say, "We've kind of seen a turn in society. In years past police officers were respected, the institution of policing was respected, and that has sort of eroded over the years. It has eroded to such a point that I'm finding it difficult to hire and recruit new police officers, and that is problematic. Now I will admit that over the years there have been incidents, or events in police history that have shaken the confidence of the public, and those are deplorable incidents that have occurred. But they have been addressed, and changes made.

"At the same time we've seen society change with a shift in a lack of respect for police officers. We've also seen that same shift and lack of respect for parents, clergy and for our elders and seniors. It seems that we're kind of losing our grip as a society over what we hold dear and near to us. The police are our last line of defense. We're the ones that are trying our darndest to keep from sinking into total chaos, and those officers need to have that support, they need to have that reinforcement. Mr. Cannon and his efforts really mean a lot to the force, and they mean a lot to me."

Chapter 8

Working

Thomas Cannon and his sons (Family Photo)

Tom Cannon was always a hard worker. When he was young he helped to support his mother and himself, and later when he had his own family he was always concerned about making enough money to support them. He worked whenever he could, at whatever job he could find. When he was in high school he worked nights and when he was at Hampton Institute and teaching in the Richmond Public Schools, he worked during summer breaks.

One summer when he was still a student at Hampton he saw an ad in the paper for temporary workers at Deep Water Terminal on the James River in Richmond, so he signed up. So did his friend Ben Wigfall, and both of them ended up having unusual experiences.

Big ships from all over the world came to that dock to be unloaded and their contents transferred to trucks to be transported elsewhere. One day both Ben and Tom were working with big bags of brown sugar that were being unloaded from a ship. Tom was unloading the bags and was down in the hold of the ship and placing them on pallets to be lifted up out of the hold, and Ben was at the other side of the shipyard loading the bags into boxcars.

Tom says, "This one time we had just finished loading the pallet, and I was walking across the hold to get some water. I was actually standing on top of the sugar bags when someone hollered a warning to me. I turned

127

to look to see what was going on, and was hit by the pallet that the winch operator was lifting up out of the hold. Normally he pulled the load to the center of the hold and then stopped and hoisted it straight up. But this particular time when he was pulling it from the end of the ship he lifted it up high enough for it to swing. So it was in motion when they hollered at me.

"It was moving so fast I didn't have time to get out of the way, and it hit me and knocked me down. I was standing on top of the sugar, and there was this little depression where there were no bags of sugar, it was just the size of a man – almost like a little grave, and I fell down in that little area. All the weight of the pallet dropped down on top of me, but it didn't touch me because the sugar bags on each side of me caught the weight of the load. If it hadn't been for that space and the pallet had landed on top of me, I would have been crushed. But as it happened it didn't hurt me at all – just scared me half to death."

Wigfall was out of sight and didn't know what had happened until afterward. His experience was not as dangerous as Tom's, but it was educational. He was loading the brown sugar bags into the boxcar and said, "I worked there for about two weeks. It was very hard, hot work, and I learned a lot in that very short time. Apparently they had the work force organized to fit the number of bags of sugar they had. In other words if they had 1,000 bags they would probably have 100 men working. As the bags went down they would cut the men, but I didn't know that. There were some older men there who did know the system. I remember I came into the job all enthusiastic and thinking that the thing was to get the job done, so I tried to load those bags as fast as possible. The bags were very heavy, they probably weighed 375 pounds each. We had a man on each corner, and we had to swing them up into piles in the boxcar. As the stack in the car got higher, we had to swing them up higher. You had to do this in a rhythm, and I was moving too fast.

"At one point everybody else just froze, and it threw me out the door of the boxcar down onto the railroad tracks. I never will forget it because the tracks were hot, and the brown sugar bag had busted open, and there were bees all around me. I was looking up at this old man standing in the door of the boxcar who explained to me I was going to run them out of a job working so fast. Everybody was aware of that strategy except me."

Tom also did seasonal work at the post office for several years. Every year about a month before Christmas the Post Office would advertise for temporary clerks and letter carriers. He said, "In college, at Christmas break, I used to go down and sign up to work. There would be a whole line of people signing up – students and anybody who could qualify. I worked at least three years as a temporary worker. One year I was a letter carrier and had my own route. Another time I worked on a truck delivering mail with a guy from Virginia State College. We worked wherever they needed you. Other people worked inside in parcel post. So I began doing postal work before I formally applied for the job. In fact, I didn't formally apply for it until a couple of years after I dropped out of teaching."

After Tom left teaching he worked for Everett Waddey, an office supply firm, and then he was hired as a porter at the Virginia Food Dealers, which was sort of like a grocer's union. There was a black preacher who was also a porter there. Until Tom was hired and became the junior porter, the preacher had to go to the liquor store and buy gin for one of the ladies who worked at Virginia Food. Tom says, "As soon as they hired me, he didn't have to run that errand anymore. I didn't mind, she was a nice person, only she had that weakness for gin. But it amused me that the rev got off the hook when I became the junior porter because he didn't like the chore of having to go to the liquor store. He didn't want any of his congregation seeing him there thinking he was buying that gin for himself."

Something exciting happened while he was working at the Virginia Food Dealers Association - he sold two of his cartoons. He only got $5.00 each for them, but he was delighted to sell his work.

The first one he sold was about the Perishable Agricultural Commodities Act. The Virginia Food

Dealers Association was against the act because it benefited the big grocery chains, and seemed to discriminate against the small grocers. That cartoon was published in the *Virginia Foodsman* magazine. And then he sold another one.

While he was in college, and even before, Tom had thoughts of becoming a professional cartoonist and submitting his work to magazines. His cartoons were comments on daily events. When he was young they were about his jobs in Chase City and Navy life. Then he began to express his opinions about national and world affairs through his cartoons. One of the early ones he did was a cartoon about the United Nations. It showed an Arab and a Jew in a boxing ring fighting. He also drew some about President Truman. One dated 1948 showed Truman in a boxing ring with a donkey holding his hand up with a little sign saying "November election finals."

When he was still a student at Hampton he went to see the editor of the *Norfolk Journal and Guide*, the local newspaper, about a job as a political cartoonist. He said, "I drew some samples of political cartoons, but nothing ever came of that. The editor said I wasn't knowledgeable enough to draw political cartoons. I championed the underdog – the little guy – in my cartoons, and I got a lot of pleasure in them. That was also a way to get a lot of emotion off my chest. I did one of a taxpayer with nothing left but a fig leaf and titled that 'Nature Boy.'

One of my favorites showed a burglar who had broken into this establishment and he turned the TV on because he didn't want to miss his favorite program *Dragnet*, and while he was watching the program the cops got him."

He continued, "I've been doing cartoons all my life – ever since elementary school. First I copied them from comic books, and eventually I started creating my own little characters. Although I was studying art, I wasn't deep into fine arts. I wasn't one of those people to say, 'I'd give my life for my art.' I never took it that seriously. It was just one way of expressing my feelings, and I prefer to express myself in a variety of ways. Sometimes with a painting or cartoon, sometimes with poetry or an essay. I would be bored to death if I just had one form of expression. But that's not the way to become a professional artist. You have to focus on one form."

While he was working for the Virginia Food Dealers he was also moonlighting at the American Tobacco Company. Each September, after the tobacco had been harvested, they hired workers to unload the tobacco from boxcars and put it on forklifts that took it up to the second floor where women were stemming the leaves. Unloading the tobacco was hard, heavy work, but the women also had a hard job as pulling the stems off the leaves was dusty and dirty work. His boss at Virginia Food Dealers got angry at Tom once or twice because after working until midnight at the Tobacco Company he was kind of lethargic, and didn't have much energy left for his day job.

Eventually his job changed at American Tobacco. He got a job oiling the machinery in the stemmery where the women were working. He said, "That was a 'gravy' job. No more huffin' and puffin' and lifting that tobacco out of the boxcars. I don't know how I got that oilers job. It didn't pay as much money, but the work was a lot easier."

While he was working in the stemmery he was impressed by the strength and determination of the women workers. He did a charcoal sketch of a working woman that was sort of a composite of the women in the stemmery. That sketch has almost become his trademark. Even today people who get letters from him see the sketch of the woman on his stationary and in stamps he attaches to the outside of his letters.

He decided to leave the job at the Food Dealers because he could see he wasn't going anywhere there. As he says, "I applied to the Postal Service because that's where the money and benefits were. A Federal job was a prime job, especially for blacks. The salary was good for that time, and the health benefits were excellent. So that was a bread-and-butter decision – a way to better provide for my family. There was no future for me at the Virginia Food Dealers. I would have been a porter as long as I was there."

So he applied for a full-time job with the Postal Service, and took the test to qualify to work there. He began working in the parcel post section in the main Richmond Post Office on the night shift because the pay was better for that shift. Once he began working at the post office, Princetta quit working and stayed home with the children. He made sure she had enough money to buy anything she wanted or needed.

Working in the parcel post section of the post office was hard physical work. The mail, mostly packages and magazines, had to be separated into sacks, and then he had to load the sacks on what they called "nutting" trucks. They were like a handcart – a flatbed cart with four wheels and an iron railing that the mail was stacked up against. They pushed that wherever the mail had to be taken.

Trucks would come in to take the mail out on the rural routes, and he'd have to take the sacks of mail downstairs and load them on a big tractor-trailer truck.

During this time his boys were students in elementary school. He spent as much time as he could with them, and even started a special club for them and the other boys in the neighborhood. His youngest son, Calvin, was interested in space and building things, so Tom built a rocketship for him. Tom said, "I went to the Goodwill Store and bought an old wheelchair and took the back off. That just left the seat with the wheels. Then I got a big old smokestack tube and used that for the body of the rocketship. It had a little cockpit that the kids could sit in with some things that spun around to look like controls. I also created a little missile that was about three-feet long with a tiny motor in the nose cone, and if you pressed a button it would spin around."

His son Thomas, Jr. remembers, "The rocketship was a pretty good sized thing – about two and a half feet in diameter and seven or eight feet long. The kids in the neighborhood heard about it and used to come around to see it. Finally this one guy who was in a gang that was called 'Hell on Wheels' because they rode bikes asked my daddy if he could form some kind of club for the kids, and he did. He made my brother an officer, but I had to start from the bottom and work my way up because daddy didn't feel it would look right for both of us to be officers. Since my brother was interested in space, he made him commander of the Flight and Missile Section."

Tom said, "I had no idea of starting a club, I just made that rocketship and missile for my two boys to play with. Kids from across the street who played with my boys came over and one of the small boys told his big brother about this big rocketship, and he came over to look at it too. Then when he asked me to organize a club for his brother and cousins, I thought it might be a good thing to do. I thought if it took this boy out of the gang he was in it might keep him out of trouble. The boys in the neighborhood were rough little kids. Some of them were from homes with no fathers, so the club became a way of sharing my fatherhood with them.

"It started out with nine boys including my two. I went to a war surplus store on Broad Street and bought them little khaki uniforms, helmet liners, canteens, and Army belts. I got them toy rifles from Woolworth's Five and Dime store. I organized them and trained them in military drills, which I had learned while I was both in the Navy and later when I was in the Army ROTC at Hampton Institute. When I graduated from Hampton, I was a second lieutenant in the Army. The name of the club was UNISCO – United Nations Interplanetary Space Command. There were two sections, and I designed different insignia for their helmets. One section was the Space Infantry section and the other the Flight and Missiles section."

Some people thought they were Boy Scouts at first, but Tom said those kids didn't have any respect for Boy Scouts because they felt that Scouts weren't tough enough and they wanted to be thought of as tough guys. So he thought about the Army infantry. The fighting soldier was considered tough, and since the space program was just getting started at that time he decided to combine the two. The club became a combination of the military and the space program.

He said, "That's how it started, it was just supposed to be a little fun thing for my sons and their friends. But it eventually got out of hand because too many kids were coming around to join it, and I didn't have the heart to turn them away. One day a little boy came to the door and he said, 'Mister, can I join that thing?' He didn't even know what it was, but he wanted to be a part of it. At one point I had 44 boys in it, and that was way too many. In the beginning I bought uniforms for all of them, but then when it got so big the fellow who left his gang and was our first Astro-commander, suggested that he and the boys start paying dues, a quarter a week. With the money from those dues we were able to buy uniforms and toy rifles for the kids who couldn't afford them.

Princetta helped with the club too. She was the club treasurer. She also used some of her own personal money to buy one of the boys some clothes.

Thomas, Jr. remembers, "We had two fully uniformed football teams and two fully uniformed baseball teams. That was pretty much unheard of back then. Most of the teams we played didn't have uniforms. My daddy bought them for all the kids. I think we might have done some small fund-raising projects, and some of the money from the dues we paid helped pay for some of them, but for the most part Daddy paid for the uniforms. Our football team was pretty good, but I think the baseball team probably lost every game we played except one. We had a good time, but there was a lot of arguing. If somebody made a mistake then the others would carry on about how stupid it was. There were some good athletes on the team, and I think some of them ended up playing high school sports, but we just couldn't click as a team."

There is one incident Tom still laughs about when he remembers the club's baseball team. Cannon says, "David was our catcher, and in this one game there was a kid on third base from the other team. So for some reason David got up from behind home plate and was bending down to dust it off, but he hadn't called time out. The man who was coaching at third gave his player the signal to run for home, and that kid came barreling down that third base line like a train. David had his back to him and was still bending over brushing off home plate and didn't see him coming. He really got trampled. I saw it happening, but there was nothing I could do. I guess David thought he had given the time-out signal, but he hadn't. When it was all over the boys were laughing and having a good time teasing him. And that's what I wanted. I wanted them to have a good time. It was just a game. So what if you lost – the world wouldn't end."

There was another incident that wasn't quite so pleasant that Tom remembers from that time. "Some of the boys lived in the West End of town, so one day I took all the boys who lived around us, and we marched from the East End to the West End to meet those guys who were members. On the way home we decided to cut back through Highland Park. Racism was pretty bad back then, and we passed a white playground.

"When those white kids saw those little black kids in their uniforms they came running out to the street and attacked us. They started throwing sticks and stones at us. I didn't know that region. If I had known what the situation was over there and the hostility that existed, there I never would have taken them through there. We went into a Safeway grocery store for protection, and I called the mother of one of the boys in the club to let her know what was going on. I also called the police. A police officer drove up in his patrol car, and I told him what the situation was and he told me 'We can't follow you around and protect you.'

"Now at this same time the police had been shadowing me in the East End because I was active in Civil Rights affairs, sending letters to the editors and going to rallies and protests, and they were a little suspicious of our military club with those ten to twelve-year-old boys marching around with their toy guns. I guess they felt I was going to ferment some kind of revolt with those boys and their toy rifles. Sometimes I would go to the front door, and there was a squad car parked across the street watching my house, and then when we needed a police car following us, he told us he couldn't do that. So I said, 'All right, then we'll protect ourselves,' and we would have, but he finally said, 'Well you go ahead, and I'll keep an eye on these guys.' As we went down the street we looked back and saw the kids around the patrol car, and they were whooping and hollering. When the patrol car left they started trailing us, but when we got to the bridge connecting the North Side with the downtown area, that kid's mother and her boyfriend arrived in their truck, and he had his pistol with him. They saw the truck roll up, and they backed off. We got the kids in the truck and got out of there. But that could have been more serious than it was because Thomas, Jr. did get hit in the head with a rock. Fortunately he was wearing his helmet liner, so it didn't do much damage.

"If anybody had told me at that time that I would end up giving money away through my philanthropy, I would have told them they were crazy. But I was giving something more important than money away then. I was giving of my physical self to those boys – and it nearly killed me."

Working all night at the post office, and then working during the day with the boys' club did take its toll on Tom. One night at work he got dizzy, and his doctor told him it was vertigo and caused by overwork and not getting enough rest. So he had to cut back on time spent with the club. At that time he also learned that there were some people who didn't understand someone trying to do something good for other people, especially where money was involved. One of the boys told Tom's younger son, "Well, at least my dad's not stupid enough to spend his money on other people's children."

Thomas, Jr. says that all of them benefited from being in the club and that discipline was the biggest thing they learned. Learning the different military drills also gave some of the boys who went into the cadet corps in high school an advantage over others, and later when he went to Virginia State and had to take ROTC he ended up joining the drill team.

His younger brother Calvin echoes his sentiments. He says, "We learned a lot in that club. Giving orders, taking orders - it was all-important. And for some of those kids it gave them a chance to belong to something. To participate in something positive."

During those years Tom was also very involved in the Civil Rights movement, which was what drew some of the police attention to him. Not that he made speeches or participated in any riots or violent demonstrations, but he gave his support to the movement by attending rallies and writing letters to the editors of the newspapers in Richmond. He felt that the movement was a young people's thing so he stayed more on the sidelines. But he did attend the two big marches on Washington, the first in which Dr. Martin Luther King delivered his *I Have a Dream* and also the Poor People's March on Washington some years later.

He also showed his support for the movement by wearing dashikis that he made. Since the dashiki was sort of the uniform of the Black Civil Rights movement he bought himself a sewing machine and taught himself to sew so that he could make his own. He took apart a dashiki that he had purchased, and used it as a pattern to make his own. He says, "I made a dashiki that was orange and I stenciled black panthers all over it. The

Black Panther Party was in existence then, and considered extremely radical. I was at Monroe Park during this demonstration there against the Vietnam War and this young white fellow in a suit with close cropped hair (I presumed he was a Federal Agent or something) started asking me about the dashiki I was wearing. I told him I made this myself, and even before he got to ask the question that I knew was on his mind I said, 'No I'm not a member of the Black Panther Party.'"

Then one day one of Tom's fellow workers at the post office pointed out a vacancy listed on the bulletin board for the railway mail service. He said, "Why would I want to do that?'" She replied, "Well it's more pay. It's a level 6 job." "When she mentioned more pay my ears perked up."

So he applied for the railway mail service and got the job, and that was the beginning of five years on the road. There was a special postal car that was like a little mobile post office, and they worked mail on the train just like they did at the post office putting it into the proper slots and then into bags. If they were "working local," they also had to drop mail off and pick it up at the stations they went through. They had to catch the mail sacks on the fly since the train didn't stop at all the stations.

Tom remembers, "We'd go barreling through these little towns and there was a crane beside the railroad tracks where they would hang their sack of outgoing mail. There was an iron hook across the door of the postal car and just before we got there we'd stop working our letters, go to the door, put goggles on, take that iron hook and when we got almost to that crane we swung that hook out and caught the pouch of mail and swung it into the postal car. At the same time we threw off the mail we'd prepared for that community. We exchanged mail on the fly, sometime that train was going 100 miles an hour. Sometimes the hook would hit that pouch so hard it would knock it out of the catcher's arms and you'd miss it. When that happened they had to put it on a truck and drive it down to the next station. Most of the time we caught it. Some of those guys were veterans out there. They were so good they could catch that mail almost blindfolded.

"But, one of the guys told me about someone who got hit by the hook, and that scared me, so I took a motorcycle helmet with me. They had a little glass window at the side of the door so you could peek down the track to see where the crane was without the cinders hitting you in the eye. When it was my turn to catch the mail off the crane, I would put my helmet on. They made fun of me and called me a sissy, but I didn't care what they called me. I was looking out for my head. Sticking my head out that door with that train flying like that - I wasn't taking any chances."

He enjoyed being on the rails because once he finished working the mail he could watch the scenery go by, and Tom enjoyed seeing the seasons change from the train. He didn't enjoy seeing the sad little groups of people waiting at some of the country stops crying and hugging each other as they waited for the coffins carrying their loved ones to be unloaded. That was right at the height of the Vietnam War, and he often looked back and saw them unloading a flag draped coffin from the baggage car. He was also on trains carrying tanks, weapons and all kinds of armament on flat cars down to Florida during the Cuban Missile Crisis. Evidently the weapons were being moved down to Florida in preparation to attack Cuba in case Russia didn't withdraw their missiles as President Kennedy had demanded.

He said, "We also hauled the Army payroll to the Army base in Fayetteville. We took the money to Washington, D.C. A helicopter used to escort the train into the station when we got near Fayetteville. We had little .38 caliber pistols – just like the old Wild West, we were supposed to defend that money with those little pistols. When we took the money to Washington, they would send a guard with a shotgun. He would sit on top of the sacks of money with his shotgun until the train left the station. This one guy in particular was funny because he was telling us, 'This shotgun will take down nine men with one blast.' Next thing you know he's up on top of the money snoring away. He wasn't going to take anybody down asleep up there. But that experience was one that I'm glad I had."

When the Postal Service phased out the train mail-cars, Tom went back to work at the main post office. It wasn't long before he developed back trouble, which eventually resulted in surgery. He said, "After my back surgery I had to lie flat on my back in bed for a while, and Princetta really took good care of me."

When he went back to work at the post office with automation and the new letter sorting machines there were fewer opportunities to make extra money working overtime. But he still was prepared to send both boys to college when they graduated from high school.

They both started at Virginia State in Petersburg, Virginia. Thomas, Jr. majored in chemistry but after two and a half years he dropped out. He says, "I lost interest in chemistry and really didn't know what I wanted to do. I wasn't doing that well and my father told me I could go back for another semester, but that if I didn't do better with my grades I would be gone. I was struggling, so I decided to drop out and was hoping to get a job as a lab technician and thought that might rekindle my interest in chemistry. But I was never able to get a job in that field." He ended up working in a totally different field and became a draftsman for a steel company.

His brother Calvin also went to Virginia State. He was majoring in microbiology, but as he says, "I wasn't too focused on school and dropped out after a year and a half, and then I got drafted by the Army."

By the early 1970's with both boys out of the house

and on their own, Tom's financial burdens eased up a bit. There was a young man living near him who could barely see. He was legally blind. Tom read about a doctor in New York who had developed a type of eyeglasses that would help people like him, but they cost $1,000 and the young man couldn't afford them. So Tom decided he would be willing to pay for them, and talked to him about sending the money to the doctor for him. But he didn't want Tom to do that. He didn't want the glasses. Tom says, "I think he was perfectly happy getting his disability checks. He couldn't work because he couldn't see. If he could see, he might have to get a job, and I don't think he wanted any part of that."

But that offer to buy special eye glasses for the boy next door planted the idea of giving away $1,000 in Tom's mind, and months later when he began his philanthropy he wrote most of his checks for $1,000.

His first philanthropic gift came about because a newspaper article informed him about a group of white women who were members of the Westhampton Junior Woman's Club helping at a neighborhood school and providing cultural and enrichment activities for the children. He became interested in their project. He learned that not only were the women providing art supplies and taking the children on field trips, but that they were including the mothers in the outings and activities. He felt that they were setting a good example for people and wanted to show his appreciation of their efforts in some tangible way.

Earlier his son Thomas had made an honorary "soul brother certificate" for one of the men he worked with at Bethlehem Steel. That was when many businesses were integrating their workforces, and some white men seemed to accept and befriend the new black employees more readily than others. So because Thomas, Jr. felt this particular white man was friendly and nice to work with he joked with him and said, "You know man, you're OK. I think I'll make you an honorary soul brother." As Thomas Jr. says, "He thought I was joking so I decided to make him a certificate. I drew one up and gave it to him, and he was very proud of it. I see him occasionally and he still has the certificate."

Tom remembered the certificate and asked his son if he minded if he changed it a little and sent it to some women. He replaced the picture of Thomas, Jr. that was on the certificate with a drawing that he made of a woman, and turned the certificate into an honorary soul sister certificate which he sent to the members of the women's club. He also included a $1,000 check to help them in their efforts.

Looking back he says, "I was impressed with what those women were doing, and I appreciated what they were doing. So I decided to do something tangible to show my appreciation. There was no flash of lightning, roll of thunder or booming voice from above telling me to start a philanthropy. That gift was an impulse – just something I decided I'd do."

Chapter 9

Philanthropist, Humanitarian or Altruist?

May 1, 2000

Dear Mr. Millsaps,

In the Saturday, April 29 edition of the Richmond Times–
Dispatch I read the article by staff writer Stacy Hawkins Adams
entitled: "Stylist gives from her heart and her hands."

The article was about Ms. Pam Williams, a professional hair-
stylist who voluntarily uses her time and talent to serve the needy
residents of Grace Home free-of-charge.

Ms. Williams is the personification of love-in-action. She is a
very wonderful woman – a God-inspired humanitarian. Therefore I
wish to pay my respects to her and express my gratitude to her as
well as the gratitude of all those residents she helps at Grace Home. I
offer and hope she will accept the enclosed check in the amount of
$1,000. There are no conditions attached to the money, she may use it
in any manner she chooses.

Ms. Stacy Hawkins Adams writes that Ms. Pam Williams is "a
powerful example of the humility, sacrifice and love of Jesus,
Gandhi, and Mother Teresa." I wholeheartedly agree with her eval-
uation of Ms. Williams' big, caring and love-filled heart.

Please do me a big favor (again) and convey my thanks to Ms.
Adams for bringing Ms. Williams' fine charitable work to my attention. Also, I would appreciate it very much if she will do me a big
favor (again) and present this check to Ms. Pam Williams with my
blessings. Thank you very much for considering my request.

Very cordially yours,
Thomas Cannon

L ike many people who receive monetary gifts from Thomas Cannon, Pam Williams thought he was a wealthy man. Even though Stacy Hawkins Adams explained to her that he was a Richmond postal worker when she delivered the check, Pam thought that he had invested in the stock market and made a lot of money that way. It never occurred to her that a man of modest financial means would give away $1,000 checks to people he didn't know.

The media have labeled him "The Poor Man's Philanthropist" and a philanthropist is defined in most dictionaries as *a person, especially a wealthy one, who practices philanthropy.* It is when you look up philanthropy that the definition comes closer to what he does because that usually states, *a desire to help mankind,* and that certainly applies to Tom. But that part of the definition is followed by, *especially as shown by gifts to charitable or humanitarian institutions,* and while he has given gifts to organizations or institutions, his gifts are usually made to individuals. Using a dictionary definition he probably comes more under the definition for humanitarian, *someone with a direct concern with promoting the welfare of humanity,* or the definition of altruistic, *putting the welfare of others before one's own interests, and therefore stressing freedom from selfishness.* He doesn't care how people define what he does, he just wants people to know that he values people over money, and that while the $1,000 he gives to people is important and may help them through a special crisis, it is the fact that he cares about them and wants to offer his support that is his real gift. He often sends a letter with his check enclosing inspirational poems or sayings to help people through a rough time.

Some people think he is crazy, while others accuse him of trying to buy his way into Heaven. He says, "A lot of people don't understand what I do and think I'm an oddball. They think I should be more like them and fit in with the norm. But if I was like them there would be no philanthropy."

Not many people would consider living in a house in a poor neighborhood without central heat, air conditioning or a telephone, and working overtime so that they could save money to give away. But that is what he did for a number of years in the beginning of his philanthropic efforts. In 1995 an article in the *Globe* called him "Saint Thomas" because he lived in near poverty, never making more than $25,000 a year. Yet between 1972 and 1995 had given $70,000 away in $1,000 gifts to teenagers, homeless people, immigrants, and those struggling to pursue an education, all while supporting and caring for his own family. He intended to stop making gifts when he retired from the post office because he knew his income would be greatly reduced. And for six years he did stop making monetary gifts. But in 1990 there was an article in the newspaper about a disabled athlete he had wanted to give a gift to years before. He had not been able to get in touch with that man then, but the article provided him the information he needed to give him a $1,000 check, so he started making gifts again. With the help of some donations from those who know of his efforts, he continues to make gifts even though he is living on his retirement income – about half of what his salary was. By the end of 2003 he had made 137 gifts and given away $144,100.

Most people who make more money than Tom would not consider making such gifts unless it was to a family member or close personal friend. But Tom's gifts are often to people he doesn't know and usually never meets. Sometimes his recipients don't even try to contact him to thank him for the gift, and on one or two occasions his chosen recipient has refused his gift. But that doesn't matter to him. He has been asked over and over by newspaper reporters, television reporters, and others who interview him why he keeps giving money away.

To answer these people he has created a list of 18 reasons why he gives money away:

1. I must give just as I receive – I have been receiving from others all my life.

2. To thank God and humanity for all lessons taught and blessings bestowed on me.

3. To show appreciation to my nation and state for educating me by way of WWII G.I. Bill of Rights and state teacher scholarships.

4. To emphasize that monetary/material values should be

subordinated to spiritual values – that which is permanent.

5. To emphasize the fact that PEOPLE are infinitely more important than money or any other material commodity or consideration.

6. To demonstrate personally how people should care for and show concern and compassion for each other without regard to racial, religious, color, national, political, ideological, or sexual consideration.

7. To demonstrate "brotherhood of man under fatherhood of God" philosophy and thus help to promote universal peace and brotherhood.

8. To teach against the excessive attachment to money and all other material treasures and sensual pleasures which delude and entrap us.

9. To help promote interracial, interreligious, and international peace and understanding.

10. To help promote the Nazarene's teaching as to how people ought to regard each other – "Love ye one another even as I have loved thee."

11. To inspire people, to encourage them to have faith in themselves – to value themselves notwithstanding handicaps of poverty and illiteracy.

12. To help restore faith among those who have lost faith in the basic goodness of human nature.

13. To demonstrate that POVERTY – like WEALTH – represents a state of specialized experience which has many valuable lessons to teach one.

14. To comfort and boost the morale of those afflicted with catastrophic illnesses, and those who must care for them.

15. To reward and inspire those who labor selflessly for others.

16. To encourage people to share their blessings with those less fortunate than they.

17. To further my own development toward detachment from money and other transient and illusory attractions of this material world.

18. To put into practice those principles of humanitarianism I am learning in the process of expanding my own conscious state of awareness

And for any and all OTHER REASONS I may choose to use.

Numbers 15 and 16 probably apply to the gift Tom gave to Pam Williams as she was giving of her time and talents to people less fortunate than she. The story written by Stacy Hawkins Adams in the *Times-Dispatch* revealed that Williams, who is a professional hair stylist, had been spending her Thursdays at Grace Home, an adult home located on Grace Street. She had been washing, cutting, perming and dyeing the hair of the men and women who lived there for two years, and never charged anything. Most of the people she worked with had some type of physical or mental disability, and Williams had been bringing her own supplies with her each week to a room in the basement of Grace Home that was designated for her use.

Tom says, "I was impressed by her caring for these men and women, and appreciated her using her hairdressing skills to cheer them up. She was doing with her hands what I was trying to do with my checks."

Williams remembers that Adams brought the check from Tom to her while she was working at Grace Home. "She read me the letter from him and handed me the check, and all these residents were sitting there waiting to get their hair done, and I burst into tears. I couldn't believe he had sent me that check. Everything I did I funded myself, so I definitely could use the money. My first thought was to use the money to buy a van to take the residents of Grace Home out to different events, but then I realized that it was exactly the amount of money I owed my therapist, so I used it to pay off that bill rather than bring it into my recent marriage.

"I had a very abusive childhood and was seeing a therapist about that, and since I was in nursing school at the time of my therapy, the doctor let me run up my bill because I wasn't able to make enough money while I was going to school to pay him. So when Mr. Cannon gave me that check, I cried and cried. His check came at such a good time."

While in nursing school Williams developed fibromyalgia and wasn't able to finish her studies. Fibromyalgia is a widespread muscular/skeletal disorder with pain and fatigue. It attacks the muscles, ligaments, and tendons. In other words Williams hurts all over and tires easily. So far medicine and treatments haven't helped, but she is now trying a vegetarian diet.

Making other people happy by using her skills as a hairdresser has helped Williams forget about her own pain and problems for a while. Williams says, "I get my relief by helping people, and working at Grace Home was one way to do that. It was funny the way that newspaper article came about. I saw a story in the paper about a woman who had been wealthy, but her family threw her out and she was living in her car. I called up the newspaper, and I just wanted to find out how to get in touch with her so I could invite her over for a meal, and tell her she could pull her car up in my driveway and sleep there anytime. I wanted to be her friend, but I never heard from her. But when I called the paper I told them, 'Just so you know I'm not a creep or a stalker, I do hair for the residents at Grace Home.' When they heard that, they wanted to interview me, and I agreed because I though maybe other hairdressers would come to help if the article was written." After the article appeared in the newspaper some other hairdressers did call Williams and come to help her at Grace Home a few times. But she was disappointed that none of them really came back for any length of time.

Still, she says, "So much good came out of that article. It led to the remodeling of the room we used. I got a brand-new roller cart and a brand-new chair that made the people more comfortable because they could lean back and be shampooed just like in a regular beauty parlor."

Williams never received any pay from the residents, but her rewards came in other ways. She says the residents called their time with her "Pam's coffee klatch" and told her they loved to come in to see her because she listened to them and made them feel important. She often sang gospel songs with them, and they had little snacks together. After she did one woman's hair the woman told her to go look in the top drawer of the dresser in her room and take the gloves that were there. They were opera-length white, silk gloves, and the woman wanted Williams to have them for her wedding. Others simply gave her hugs and expressions of love. She says, "They appreciated everything I did for them. Many of them had family that didn't bother to visit them, so they really appreciated the attention I gave them. They were so thankful to know that I cared about them."

Grace Home is now closed, and the residents dispersed to other facilities. But Williams has fond memories of the time she spent there, and the check that Tom sent her in recognition of her work at that time. Now that she knows that he is not a wealthy man she is even more thankful for his gift and says, "I just want to give him a big hug, and take him one of my husband's homemade apple pies."

Chapter 10

Postal Worker

November 1981 (Photo: Sam Henderson)

The sound of paper ripping jarred Tom back to awareness. He was at his station on the main floor of the main post office, and the monotony of the work and the constant, repetitive sound of the sorting machines had lulled him into a semi-sleep state. That was not uncommon for those who worked the graveyard shift.

When he worked mail on the train men often fell asleep because the clickey-clack of the wheels hitting the rails, and the rocking motion of the train made it hard to stay awake. As he says, "Some of those men would fall asleep on the train while working their mail standing up, and mail would fly everywhere. If you fell asleep you had to hope your buddy who was working next to you would catch you before you hit the floor. That never happened to me, but I lived off No-Doz most of the time I worked for the post office."

This particular night on the post office floor he had started to fall asleep, and he found himself holding a letter that was somebody's utility bill, and he had started to open it. He immediately reported the incident to his supervisor, so he didn't suffer any repercussions. The only reason he could think of that he might be opening a letter that was not addressed to him was that people had heard about his recent $1,000 gifts, and they had started writing to him asking for money. The clerks at the post office knew that, and whenever they found a letter addressed to the "money man" or "the man who gives money away," they got it initialed by their supervisor and brought it directly to him. So he had been opening his own letters at work, and in his dazed state must have thought that was what he was doing that night.

He says, "I'm glad there were no postal inspectors on the catwalk that night or they might have wondered what was going on." The catwalk was an enclosed area below the ceiling that traversed the main floor, and there were slots in the walls so people working on the floor below could be observed. Periodically, or whenever any irregularities were suspected, the postal inspectors monitored the floor from that catwalk. But Tom's supervisors knew that he would never do anything illegal like open mail to remove a check or money. Two of his past supervisors had nothing but praise for his hard work and dedication.

Robert Snead, who has retired from the post office, says he always found Tom to be a good worker who did his job without complaining, and was always very reliable.

Charlotte Adkins, another co-worker, says he was very quiet and always kept to himself. "When you have a lot of employees there are usually little groups that congregate, and he wasn't a part of that. He kept to himself, and I never heard anything bad out of his mouth about anybody or anything. There are usually a lot of gossips in the workplace, but he never participated in any of that. He always did his job and went about his own business."

Hard as it was to stay awake, many of the years he worked for the post office Tom worked the graveyard shift, from midnight to 8 a.m. He did that for two reasons. The first was that most businesses were only open during the day, and if he worked nights then he could go pay his bills and take care of things he needed to attend to when he got off work. If he worked in the daytime, everything would be closed by the time he got off. The other reason was that working the night shift paid more, and Tom worked that shift and as much overtime as he could so that he could save money for what he called his "peculiar hobby" of giving away $1,000 checks.

After he made that first gift of a thousand dollars to the Westhampton Junior Woman's Club he realized that since money was the most powerful symbol in our culture by making monetary gifts he could not only help people, but he could make a powerful statement. A statement based on his spiritual beliefs that all religions share a common root which is the Golden Rule, "Do unto others as you would have them do unto you." Along with that is his belief that each of us is a cell in the body of the cosmic consciousness. He says, "No matter what kind of body we are in – male, female, black, white, red, or brown – in essence we are all one. So by helping others I am actually helping myself."

Unfortunately he got off to a rather shaky start. His check to the Westhampton Junior Woman's Club went unnoticed in a pile of unopened mail for several weeks. In 1972, $1,000 was a great deal of money – you could buy a car for $4,000 or $5,000, and make a down payment on a decent house for $500. So Tom was rightly concerned that his $1,000 gift might have gone astray. When he didn't hear from the club, he called and asked if they had gotten his letter and mentioned that there was a check enclosed. Thinking that it was a donation of $10 or so the woman who spoke with him thanked him, and said she would look for his letter. But it took them another few days to find it and open it. Of course they were quite surprised to find that his check was for $1,000 and must have been a little embarrassed that they had treated his generous gift so carelessly. Also enclosed in the envelope were the "Honorary Soul Sister" certificates - one for each member of the club.

Since his gifts were about more than money, there was always something else tucked inside the envelope with the check. He wrote letters of support and encouragement and added copies of inspirational poems or items such as the "Soul Sister" certificates which were intended to convey the message of the importance of one human being caring about another. Many of his recipients have said that as nice as it was to receive the money, the fact that a total stranger would go to the trouble of letting them know how much he cared about them and sending them a message of encouragement was even more important than the check itself.

Poor Man's Philanthropist

His second $1,000 gift was divided between ten charitable organizations. But those were organizations that were already getting donations from the general public, and the gifts seemed rather impersonal. It was important to Tom to be able to touch a special person with his gift, so he began making gifts to people he read about in the newspaper. Stories of those who had suffered a tragic or traumatic experience, people who had shown courage in a difficult situation, helped other people, or were working particularly hard trying to get an education touched his heart and made him feel compelled to reach out to them through his letters and checks.

In May of 1973 he read about a Nigerian student at Virginia Union University who had chronic kidney failure and was on dialysis three times a week for about eight hours at a time. Although he had visual problems and suffered from constant nausea and headaches, he continued going to school as well as to a job as a guard at the Virginia Museum of Fine Arts. The student wanted to bring his wife and two children to the United States but needed sponsorship for them. Tom wrote to the reporter who wrote the article and told him that he did not have the financial security necessary to sponsor the young man's family but that he was concerned for his welfare – concerned enough to dip into his hard-earned savings and send him a $1,000 check. Tom also wrote, …*perhaps it will be of some small comfort to him to find that in the "brotherhood of man under the fatherhood of*

God" there are no strangers in a strange land. There are only __BROTHERS__, only __FAMILY__. He also praised the reporter, Sid Cassese, for bringing the story of the young man to the attention of the public and said, *...the* Richmond Times-Dispatch – *and __YOU__ particularly, Mr. Cassese, surely have performed a heart-warming act of human compassion as well as a wonderful public service.*

Later in that same month he read about an insurance agent who was going door to door collecting on his debts when he was robbed and shot. He died leaving his wife, Dixie Headley with five children to raise. Mrs. Headley also received a letter and check from Tom.

His gift to Diane Jarrelle, also in 1973, set the stage for an event he assumes had something to do with the psychic realm, but he still can't explain it. Jarrell's husband, Vernon L. Jarrelle, Jr., was shot and killed during a holdup at a Richmond food-stamp distribution center, and she was left with a young daughter and no insurance. Tom sent her a $1,000 check and of course she was extremely grateful for the money, but also appreciated the sentiments he expressed in the letter he sent. He had been studying various religions and reading about different spiritual beliefs. In an effort to soothe her grief he told her that he believed in life after death and that only her husband's earthly body had been destroyed, and that he wasn't his body.

She invited him to her home to talk, and when he and Princetta arrived they met some of her friends who were also visiting. He didn't realize that two of the women also in the room were psychics. They were sitting on either side of him as the conversation shifted to the continuation of life and his beliefs. As he talked about his belief in a Cosmic Consciousness rather than a God created in the image of man, he began to get quite worked up and rather emotional. All of a sudden one of the women next to him called out, "Did you see that?" She and the other psychic had seen a light flashing up from Tom's shoulders. They had no explanation for what they had seen, and Tom can't explain why later when his son took a picture of him there seemed to be a light entering, or coming out of, his chest in the area near his heart. Photo experts have examined the picture and say it is not a flaw in the film or a mistake in the developing process. No one has really been able to explain what is seen in the print.

He doesn't discuss his spiritual beliefs with many people because most are more in tune with organized religions, and when these subjects come up they try to change him to their way of thinking. Tom has no intention of changing and as he says, "If I thought like they did, there would be no philanthropy."

And there was no mention of spirituality when an article about him and his gift to Jarrelle, and others, appeared in *Parade* magazine.

For most people who read the article in *Parade* it was the first time they had heard of the Richmond postal worker who was giving away $1,000 checks on a salary of around $11,000 a year. But that was not the first publicity his philanthropy received.

Earlier in 1973 he had established a scholarship in the name of a student at Hampton Institute who had died. Her brother contacted Sheilah Kast, a reporter at the *Richmond News Leader*, and told her about the $1,000 scholarship Tom had awarded in his sister's name. The generosity of a man many considered "poor" interested her, and she contacted him to find out more about why he was giving his money away. Her article was the first publicity he received, and it was picked up by other papers. That is what led to other articles being written about him, and it wasn't long before he was getting calls from national newspapers and magazines wanting to know more about this man who the media eventually dubbed "The Poor Man's Philanthropist."

The publicity brought comments from his neighbors in the East End – some of them good, but many of them hurtful. Katie Bryant, who used to own and run Bryant's Market around the corner from the Cannon's home in Church Hill, knew him and his wife Princetta. She often heard people talking about Tom and saying how crazy he was, and that he shouldn't be doing what he was doing because he didn't have that much money himself. Katie says, "I'd tell them we need more people like him because he cares about people and tries to help them. I told them he wasn't crazy at all – that he was a very intelligent man."

And when she heard people saying he should take care of his own family and give his money to his wife, she'd tell them they didn't know what they were talking about because when Mr. Cannon got paid he always gave Princetta a certain amount of money and she always had whatever she needed. According to Katie, Princetta supported him 100%, and she was a very giving person too. She remembers that Princetta used to come by the store and talk with her just about every day, and sometimes she'd bring her food for lunch - a little steak or fried potatoes. She says the Cannons were both just very giving people. "If Princetta went up town to go shopping and saw a blouse or something she thought I'd like, she would bring it to me, and I'd do the same for her. She helped in the community, and so did he. If they saw a neighborhood child that needed clothes, they would buy them and give them to that child."

But Katie says a lot of people just couldn't relate to that kind of compassion or generosity. She says, "People used to say, 'You ought to tell that crazy-ass friend of yours he ought to spend his money on his own house.' People just didn't understand. I'd tell them they shouldn't talk like that. He was a very good man, doing a lot of good work – and still is."

Princetta never talked about it, but Tom feels certain that she also received criticism from other women in the neighborhood for letting him carry out his philanthropy. Just as he was not concerned with material things and did not have any expensive habits like drinking, smoking, gambling, or doing drugs, neither did Princetta. She was not interested in fancy clothes or jewelry, but she did love shoes. That was her weakness. Tom says that at one time she had 18 pairs of shoes gathering dust in her closet. But otherwise she was happy living a modest lifestyle.

Because he worked overtime and they kept to their frugal lifestyle and didn't do any entertaining, Tom was able to save money for his philanthropic efforts. Occasionally Princetta made her own philanthropic gifts. Once she used the last $800 of her personal savings to buy a new recliner chair for a disabled woman who lived next door to them. Another time she gave out $50 bills to about a dozen neighborhood women simply because she wanted to share what she had with them. But one time she got a little carried away. Tom says, "There was a young boy in our neighborhood who needed an operation and his family was requesting blood donations, so Princetta volunteered my blood. Now she didn't volunteer to donate any of her own blood, but she offered mine." Laughing, he added, "I guess I'm lucky he didn't need a heart transplant, or she might have said, 'Go on, take my husband's. He doesn't need it.' She was kind and giving, but she could be dizzy sometimes, and once she committed me to donating the blood I couldn't make her look bad by refusing to give it."

Princetta never complained about him giving away money, and neither did his sons who were grown and living on their own by that time. He says, "To this day I don't know what either one of my boys think about the philanthropy. It just doesn't come up, but I've never neglected my duties towards my family. Princetta didn't have to work after I started working at the post office and when the boys were young I spent a lot of time with them, and they had everything they needed.

"The only one who ever expressed anger at me giving money away was my brother Ben, and I didn't learn about that until after he died. I had given him a $1,000 gift, but his son told me he was angry at me for not giving him more money," Tom says. "I guess he thought I owed him something because he had done so much for me when I was a young boy. After our father died, he and my oldest brother Joe practically raised me. When I was a child I couldn't have asked for better brothers, but when they got older and got married we became estranged. It was mainly that I didn't fit the mold their wives thought I should, and I wasn't about to change to please them. Evidently when Ben read about my giving money away it annoyed him, but he never told me about it."

Publicity about Tom increased. Stories about him appeared in *Ebony* magazine, *The Reader's Digest*, and even a newspaper in Finland. People began coming to his home asking for money, and he began getting letters with similar requests.

Tom says, "When we lived in the East End people would come to the door with all sorts of sad stories. One young man in the neighborhood had gotten into drugs, and he owed the drug dealers a lot of money. He came to me looking for help because he said a contract had been put out on him, and he would be killed if I didn't come up with the money to pay off his debt. I didn't want the boy killed, but I couldn't start paying those kinds of debts. I think some of the people thought I was a one-man welfare agency. But I'd have had a line five miles long if I responded to those requests.

And he didn't respond to most of the letters he got either. One man who was in prison wrote to him saying that he was about to commit suicide – he had made a noose out of a bed sheet and fastened it to the top of his cell door, put it around his neck, climbed up on a stool, and was about to jump when a guard brought him the copy of *Ebony* with the story about Tom in it. According to him, that gave him a new lease on life, and he wanted Tom to do one of two things for him. Either send him $500 to pay his bail to get him out of jail so he could go and look for his wife and child in South Carolina, or go look for them for him. Tom says, "He didn't want much – just for me to bear the expense, and take my time to go look for his wife and child."

Another man wrote to ask if Tom could send him

$1,000 because he needed to have the tattoo of his ex-girlfriend's name removed. "I didn't answer his letter, and I don't answer these strange requests that come in the mail, but if I had answered him, I would have suggested that he keep that tattoo, and look for another girl with the same name," Tom says with a smile.

Someone else claimed to have a back problem that could only be cured at a clinic in Switzerland, but he added, "If you can't afford to send me to Switzerland, I've heard there is a clinic in Mexico that is almost as good."

One woman wrote that she needed money and she had tried prayer, but that didn't work, so she was writing to Tom. He says, "Well, prayer might work if she got up off her fanny and went out to look for a job after she prayed. God's not going to drop money down out of Heaven on her." And Tom wasn't about to either.

One lady wanted him to buy a car for her minister. She told him the minister would like to have a Cadillac or a limousine, but he would accept a Ford Mustang. Still others said he was their last hope – that they would kill themselves if he didn't send them some money.

Not all of his mail brought requests for money. One day he got a nice surprise in the mail. He had just returned from driving to New Jersey to see his younger son Calvin who had been hospitalized for an infection. Fortunately by the time he got there, Calvin was doing fine and ready to be released from the hospital. But Tom had driven up to New Jersey after working all night at

the post office and had to drive right back so he would-
n't miss work. By the time he drove back home he was
exhausted. When he walked in the door Princetta gave
him his mail, but he was too tired to deal with it. She
pointed out that one of the letters seemed to be from
the singer Roberta Flack. Thinking that it was probably
just a publicity release saying that she would be appear-
ing in town or something like that, he didn't want to
bother opening it. But Princetta persisted, so he finally
opened the letter. At that point he knew what some of
the people he had sent checks to felt like and what a
surprise it was to receive an unexpected check. Inside
the envelope was a check for $1,000 and a letter from
Flack's office manager explaining that Ms. Flack had
read the story about him in *Ebony*, and was sending him
the $1,000 gift for him to use as he saw fit and to say
"She loves you." Later he told a reporter from the
Richmond Afro-American that before that the largest
amount anyone had ever given him had been about ten
dollars, so her gift was quite a shock. As he said, "If I
hadn't had a strong heart, she might have killed me with
her 'love.'"

Of course Tom did not use the $1,000 gift from
Roberta Flack on himself. Instead, he used it for an arts
program at the state penitentiary. Claudette Black
McDaniel, who was a local radio personality and therapist at the Medical College of Virginia, had organized
craft classes for the inmates and he had been going there

every Saturday for several months. In addition to the craft classes he helped the inmates form a band. Since two of the inmates needed instruments, he used part of the money to buy a trumpet and a flute.

Tom's philanthropic efforts began on a whim and continued whenever he felt inspired to help someone he read about in the newspaper. He feels that he was actually being sent on a mission and that his giving was divinely inspired – although he did not recognize that fact immediately.

The first hint that something might be guiding his actions was a gift he made to a burn victim in Dallas, Texas. An anonymous person in Texas wrote to him and enclosed a story from a Dallas newspaper about a young girl who had been tragically burned. While he was mulling over whether or not to send her family a check he stopped at the newsstand in the post office building on his way home from work, and bought a copy of another newspaper. When he got into his car he started to look through the paper, and it fell open to a story about the same little girl.

That seemed to indicate to him that he was supposed to help this girl's family. He decided to send them a monetary gift, but he encountered problems getting that check delivered, too. Thinking that he could contact her through the reporter who wrote the story in the Dallas paper, he wrote to the reporter, but his letter was returned saying that the reporter no longer worked there. Finally he went to the library and looked up the family's name in a Dallas phone book and made contact directly with them. Eventually his check was delivered.

In 1973 he read about Hattie Kindred in the *Virginian-Pilot*, a newspaper in Norfolk, Virginia. The story related how Kindred had seven children of her own and had been looking after nine nieces and nephews since her brother died in 1962. She was a bus driver for the Southeastern Tidewater Opportunity Project (STOP) which provided transportation for poor people to community services. She also provided food, clothing and shelter for some of the young and older people in her community when they needed help, and she worked with Police Community Relations to collect donations of food from local business to serve at block parties which were attended by up to 15,000 people. When her job at STOP was phased out, she told the reporter, Patrice Owens, from the *Virginia-Pilot* that she believed everything would work out. Even so, she was completely surprised when Tom's check for $1,000 arrived. Her plans for the money included eight pairs of shoes for a neighborhood family and a queen-sized bed and a refrigerator for her family.

When Owens asked Tom why he gave money to people he didn't know, Tom told her that he had been trying to overcome the attractions of the material world and that to test his ability he decided to see if he could give away large amounts of money without harboring regrets or remorse. He added that he thought he had passed the test.

He has always said that he does not expect any thanks from those he gives gifts to and that they do not have to accept his gift. He attaches no strings to the gift, and while he might suggest the person spend the money on a vacation or something for themselves, he says they are free to do what they want with the money. He is not insulted if someone turns down a gift, because that just allows him to use that money for a gift to someone else.

And that is what happened when he made one of his more unusual gifts. He decided to honor a wealthy philanthropist who financially supported numerous Richmond charities and cultural institutions. In his letter to him, Tom stated that he knew he didn't need the money, but that he was sending him the check to show his respect for him and that he held him in high regard. The philanthropist did send the check back with a letter telling Tom how much he appreciated the thought behind his gift, and that he had made a copy of the check and framed it and had it hanging in his office. Tom then used the money to make a gift to a woman who had done a great deal of community service.

He also gave gifts to an Egyptian man who had brought his son to the Medical College of Virginia from Kuwait for medical treatments, a group of teenagers in Tidewater, Virginia, who rescued a horse that had become stuck in the mudflats of the Elizabeth River in Chesapeake, Virginia, two young girls who rescued a kitten, and a blind man and his dog.

The list of gifts began getting longer and longer, and by 1980 he had made 44 monetary gifts to individuals for scholarships, to those suffering from illness, to people who needed support through a difficult time, to recognize some for community service, and to reward honesty. He had also given to the Charlotte County Rescue Squad, the Little Sisters of the Poor, the Boy's Club of Richmond, Children, Inc., the Richmond Police, the Richmond Symphony, the Petersburg Symphony, and the governors of each of the 50 states and its territorial possessions, and the District of Columbia in his Bicentennial project. All these gifts totaled $41,485 – more than the amount of three years salary for him.

It wasn't long before he was being honored by groups around the country. His first award came in 1974 when he was awarded a Certificate of Merit by the Dictionary of International Biography in London, England. He also received a Distinguished Achievement Award from the International Biographical Center in Cambridge, England.

But even as he was receiving awards and recognition, he had moments when he wondered if he was really making a difference in the general scheme of things. He still saw people striving for money, wealth and power as if those were the important things in life. By his gifts he was trying to show the importance of people over possessions and money, how human life is infinitely more important than money and material things, but he wasn't sure he was getting his message across.

One day he was sitting on his couch in the living room feeling depressed. His mind was filled with negative thoughts. He had been reading of corruption in high office, a rising murder rate, frequent robberies. These all threw him into a state of doubt and depression. He temporarily lost faith in the goodness of human nature.

He was especially unhappy about the way people treated one another over money. Grasping for wealth, stealing, lying, and driven by greed, not realizing that in the end they had to give it all up, because in the end everyone ends up the same. He began to doubt if people were worthy of his concern and the sacrifices he was making to make his monetary gifts. And then a message came into his consciousness and told him to go upstairs and look in his box of religious scrolls. When he randomly picked out a rolled up scroll it said, *You did not choose me, but I chose you and appointed you that you should go and bear fruit and that your fruit should abide.* He did not know who the chooser was – was it God? Or was it John, because the biblical quote was from the Book of John Chapter 15, 16th verse? It didn't matter who the chooser was, the quote gave him the inspiration he needed to continue.

A few years later he began to sink into a similar depression when he again sensed a message telling him to look at his scrolls. Once he read a scroll he did not put it back in the box, so he was amazed when he pulled a scroll with the same verse on it from the box. Evidently there was more than one copy of each biblical saying, but pulling the same saying from the box twice seemed to mean that it was meant especially for him.

The last time he started to doubt his mission he received a religious magazine in the mail that someone had sent him from London, England. As he held it in his hands he noticed that one of the pages was folded up or crimped as if he was to open it at that spot. When he did, there at the top of the page was the same biblical verse, *You did not choose me, but I chose you...* After that third experience, that was enough. He never doubted his mission again, and did not need any more confirmations that he was doing the right thing.

Because he encountered a few problems trying to deliver his checks himself with some of his early gifts, he developed a method for distributing his gifts that he still uses today. When he reads a newspaper article about someone who inspires him and he feels compelled to send a gift, he contacts the editor of the newspaper. He tells them about the story he read and asks them if they would please ask the reporter who wrote the story, or someone else at the paper, to deliver the check for him.

This serves two purposes. For one thing, he can be sure that the check will get to the intended person, and by working through the editor of the paper his gift often results in a follow-up story about the person receiving the $1,000 gift. That is almost as important as the gift itself because his hope is that seeing those follow-up articles will encourage others to think of ways they can reach out to people either monetarily or through some other actions. He has always said the $1,000 is important, but it is only symbolic of his regard and respect for others, and that by giving money away he is demonstrating that people are more important than money. He hopes to spread his message and inspire others to learn that lesson and act on it – maybe not in the same way he does, but by giving of themselves to help others.

Recently Tom has been writing to Bill Millsaps, Senior Vice President and Executive Editor of the *Richmond Times-Dispatch*, and Bill has had several *Times-Dispatch* reporters deliver checks for Tom. Tom feels that newspapers such as the early *News Leader*, the *Richmond Afro-American*, and now the *Times-Dispatch* and *Richmond Free Press* have played an important role in his philanthropy, and that without them he would not have been able to help the people that he has.

He once wrote an essay called *The Tree and Me* citing how trees furnish the wood to make the paper the newspapers are printed on, the reporters write the stories that inspire him to make gifts, and the newspaper is delivered to him so that he can read about these people. He has told some of the reporters that he feels they are like his foot solders because they go out in the field and find these worthy people and write about them and that brings them to his attention. He says the reporters should receive part of the credit for his philanthropy. In sports terms, like in baseball or football, they should receive an "assist," because without them there would be no philanthropy.

He is particularly appreciative of the cooperation he has received from Bill Millsaps, and Bill says that he has been happy to be a part of Tom's efforts. Once when he sent Bill a letter and said he hoped he wasn't making a nuisance of himself, Bill wrote him back and said, *You may be certain that your generosity is not a nuisance to anyone here at the* Richmond Times-Dispatch.... *We are pleased to serve as your intermediaries and feel proud that some of our stories have inspired you to help people who are struggling.*

In a time when the newspapers are often filled with stories of murders, robberies, and war, Tom's efforts often bring a ray of sunshine into the lives of those who must report those events. Millsaps has said, "Often when the news is depressing, and things are pretty glum around the office a letter will arrive from Tom Cannon and turn our day around."

In the same way that newspapers have enabled him

to pursue his philanthropic hobby, working at the post office made it easier for him to do so. He says, "I'm almost convinced that my entry into the postal service was predestined to prepare me for this mission of giving the money away, because the giving was done primarily by mail. I could write letters and bring them to work, and put them right in the sack that was going to that location. And not only could I expedite the mail I was sending out, I got all the mail coming to the Richmond post office for me no matter how it was addressed. Many of the mail clerks were looking out for me. I got letters addressed to, 'The Money Man', 'The Black Man who gives money away', 'God's angel', and one that was just addressed to 'The Man.'"

On one occasion he had an experience that again verified his spiritual beliefs and confounded one of his co-workers. He and a fellow clerk were working beside the conveyor belt that was bringing mail that was dumped on it on a lower lever up to them to be thrown off into the proper hampers. Tom says, "I don't remember what started the conversation but I was telling this guy, 'As a man soweth, so shall he reap.' Just as I got the words out of my mouth, a large manila envelope that was coming up the conveyor belt burst open at one end and a sheaf of papers slid out of it right in front of us, and on the topmost sheet were the same words, 'As a man soweth, so shall he reap.' My coworker looked at me and his mouth fell open – he was speechless, but that was immediate confirmation of what I had just said.

"Another time at the same location, some material directly related to some experiments I had been reading about showed up on a magazine on the conveyor belt in front of me. It seems that whenever I have been interested in a particular subject I often come in contact with that material one way or another. That just verifies the statement 'Seek and ye shall find.' If you are trying to progress in the path of spirituality, you seem to have unseen assistance that you can't really explain. Not that I'm more spiritual than anybody else, but I've always seriously sought knowledge in various areas and I've received help when I needed it."

"Although working at the post office helped with his philanthropy, he never felt like he really fit in with the other employees there. Many of the workers would socialize together after work, while he went home to his family. Once when he was telling one of his fellow employees that he didn't smoke or chew tobacco, dip snuff, drink, gamble, or chase after wild women the man said, "Well, what are you living for? You might as well be dead. You're missing out on the good stuff in life." Tom says he responded, "Yes, I'm missing out on all the good stuff in life such as drug addition, alcoholism, unwanted fatherhood, and being shot by sore losers and jealous boyfriends and husbands."

Tom says he was considered an oddball, and he

remembers one man telling him that when he first started work at the post office someone told him to stay away from Tom Cannon because he's crazy. Later Tom was to write an essay entitled *Crazy Like Me* where he discussed what he thought the world would be like if everyone was crazy like him.

But as he says, "If I was so crazy, why did I start to get awards and commendations from some of the most prestigious institutions for my work?"

In 1977 he received the Award for "Humanitarian-Philanthropic Endeavors and Contributions Toward Universal Brotherhood" from the NAACP, Richmond, Virginia Branch. He received the Mike Douglas "Special People" Award in November of that year. In 1978 he received the 1977 Jefferson Award for Outstanding Service Benefiting Local Communities from the American Institute for Public Service in Washington, D. C. He was presented the Order of Michael the Archangel Knighthood Medal and Citation from the Order of Michael the Archangel Police and Fire Legion in Las Vegas, Nevada in November, 1978, and in December received the National Brotherhood Award from the National Conference of Christians and Jews, Virginia Region. He also received the Distinguished Service Award form the International Y's Men Club and a Meritorious Service Citation from the Postmaster General in Washington, D. C. in March of 1979.

He appeared on the *Mike Douglas Show* in

December, 1977, on *PM Magazine* in November, 1980, on the *Voice of America* radio broadcast, and *The American Character* on the Dr. Norman Vincent Peale radio show's Sept. 19, 1983 broadcast.

Chapter 11

An Overdue Gift

Mayor's Commission for the Disabled
City of Richmond
City Hall

Richmond, Va. 23223

Dear Sirs:

In the Richmond Times-Dispatch of Friday, October 19, I read that the Mayor's Commission for the Disabled will present its Most Distinguished Service Award to Mr. Wannie B. Cook at City Hall on Monday, Oct. 22, at 6:00 P.M. Please do me a favor and supplement that award with the enclosed gift of one thousand dollars ($1,000.00) for Mr. Cook.

During the years of 1972 -1984 when I was engaged in my philanthropic-humanitarian endeavors, my choice of recipients for $1,000 gifts was selected from several categories I had established for that purpose. One category involved the overcoming of catastrophic physical disabilities – the triumph of the human spirit over Life's adversities. Mr. Wannie B. Cook belonged in that particular category.

Years ago I tried to contact Mr. Cook to give him a $1000 check. At the time I had read that he was a business student at Virginia Union University here in Richmond. I made a phone call to Virginia Union, but he had left the campus. Because of the confidential nature of student records, I was not permitted to have his home address. Consequently, my monetary gift intended for Mr. Cook has been on hold ever since that time.

When I read that you were going to present your Most Distinguished Service Award to Mr. Cook, I knew that would be the perfect occasion to have my long-delayed monetary tribute presented to him. So please do me the big favor of serving as my inter-

mediary and supplementing your Award to Mr. Cook with the enclosed check for one thousand dollars.($1,000).

Wannie B. Cook has been one of my biggest heroes for many years. I have followed his career in the news media, and I have watched him compete in the Richmond Newspaper's Marathon events.

Whenever I think of COURAGE I think of Wannie Cook. Whenever I think of STRENGTH I think of Wannie Cook. Whenever It think of TENACITY I think of Wannie Cook. Whenever I think of CHARACTER I think of Wannie Cook. Whenever I think of WILL-POWER I think of Wannie Cook. Whenever I think of INCONQUERABLE HUMAN SPIRIT I think of Wannie Cook. Whenever I think of ROLE MODEL, for us all, I think of Wannie Cook.

For all of the above reasons and many others not mentioned, I request your permission to join the Mayor's Commission for the Disabled in honoring and saluting Mr. Wannie B. Cook by means of this monetary award I have enclosed for him. It is a relatively small token of the high esteem in which I hold him.

Very cordially yours,
Thomas Cannon

During the ceremony in the lobby of Richmond's City Hall, Wannie Cook (now known by most people as Ike Cook) was grateful and composed, as he accepted his award and the check from Thomas Cannon. An amputee who was wounded in the Vietnam War, he was recognized by the commission for encouraging other disabled people both through his work as a therapeutic recreation student at Virginia Union University and by his achievements as a local, national and international sports competitor. He helped establish the wheelchair division of the Richmond Newspaper's Marathon, and won that division ten times. But his composure dissolved as he drove home, and tears ran down his cheeks as he thought about Tom's generous gift.

Later he wrote Tom a thank-you note stating, *Sometimes when giving so much to others who are less fortunate one feels undeserving when receiving. Now that two days have passed, when the thought of your gift enters my mind, or when I speak of you, a lump develops in my throat, and I must pause for a second or two. This memory will always be cherished.*

Ike says he knew who Tom was because he had read numerous articles in the newspaper about him, but he had never met him. When he received the check, he wondered why. He says, "Actually I felt very undeserving of anybody giving me $1,000. I felt like I hadn't really done anything to earn it. I had organized some wheelchair sports teams which at that time were composed mostly of veterans, and so I took the money and donated it to our wheelchair teams."

In the 1970s there were a lot of young veterans coming out of Vietnam with various injuries and disabilities, and Ike was one of them. He was a patient at Hunter-Holmes McGuire Veterans Hospital from 1973 to 1974. That was one of four or five spinal-cord injury centers in the country, so anyone on the East Coast with that type of injury came through the Richmond hospital.

As Ike says, "We were all in-patients and we got together and decided we wanted to put together a wheelchair sports team. We were all basically lying around the VA hospital after coming back from Vietnam, and being so young we wanted more than just to be a hospitalized patient. We thought we could go into the community and make a difference. And we certainly wanted to make more out of our lives than to be just an institutionalized person. We got together and searched around the country to find out what all was available and started developing our own teams.

Basketball helped many of us, but there were some that were interested in other things. We had some that liked arts, some liked music and others were involved with archery or billiards before they were injured. We were still brand-new in wheelchairs, but we got together and said, 'Let's form a team not just for us, but for anyone who comes behind us.' At that time the VA was loaded with returning Vietnam veterans who had been injured, and when some of the men were released from McGuire they went back to their own areas, and started wheelchair sports teams there.

"I used Mr. Cannon's money for the Independent Wheelchair Athletic Association, and that way it touched a lot of people. We had some new veterans who had recently been injured that we sent to the national veteran's wheelchair games. Some of it went to snow skiing for people in wheelchairs from our local team, some of it went to the local basketball team, and some went to introducing bowling to people in wheelchairs. So his money went an extremely long way. And we were just absolutely struck with him.

We had some veterans organizations that were keeping us alive – if we needed $100 here or $100 there we could go to them, and they were more than helpful, but basically we were struggling, so to have $1,000 in our treasury – that was a whole lot for us. At that time the organization was for veterans, but now it's not restricted to veterans. We have about sixty members, but we'd like to be able to build up our junior membership."

When Ike retired from the VA hospital he coached a women's wheelchair basketball team for a number of years. He took that team from ninth to number three in the country. He started playing basketball again, and now is on two wheelchair teams.

Tom usually doesn't meet the people he gives checks to, and that's really the way he intends for his philanthropy to work. He doesn't expect the people he gives checks to keep him informed of their activities, and after he has made his initial show of support and concern for them, he doesn't feel he needs to keep reinforcing that gesture. So it was a little unusual when arrangements were made for Tom and Ike to meet on a television program.

After he retired from the post office in 1984, he stopped making monetary gifts for a while. His retirement salary was half what his regular pay had been, and he knew he would not be able to keep giving as he once had. But he says, "This philanthropy seems to have a mind of its own, and I'm just drawn along with it. When I saw the article about Wannie (Ike) Cook, I knew I had to make that long overdue gift. He stands out above all the other recipients of my checks, because if it hadn't been for him, I might not have resumed my giving."

So he kept getting publicity, and invitations to appear on television shows. People from the *Oprah Winfrey Show* called, and asked him to appear on the *Oprah Show*, but the date they had selected was a date that he had already agreed to appear at a post office event, and he wasn't about to go back on a commitment - not even for Oprah Winfrey.

Another date was scheduled and his trip to Chicago

was planned. Oprah's staff called his son Thomas and told him and his wife Jennifer that Oprah wanted to give Tom a present when he appeared on the show, and asked for suggestions. Their immediate response was that he would love to have some money to give to other people, but they were told that Oprah didn't give money to her guests, so they decided on a computer.

The producers of the show arranged for a crew in Richmond to interview Tom and some of the people he had given checks to. As a special surprise Ike Cook was contacted and arrangements made for him to go to Chicago to be on the show and meet Tom during the live portion of Oprah's show. At first Ike was hesitant, but they told him he'd be on for just a minute or two. So Tom and Ike headed to Chicago for the show, but they flew on different planes and Tom did not know that Ike was scheduled to be a part of his segment.

Oprah's staff went to great lengths to try to keep Ike's appearance a secret so that Tom would be surprised on the show. But by chance the same cab driver that took Ike to his hotel, picked Tom up at the airport. So as cab drivers do, he started talking with Tom, and asked him where he was from and why he was visiting Chicago. When Tom told him he was from Richmond and in town to be on the *Oprah Show*, the driver said something like, "What a coincidence, I just brought a man in from Richmond in a wheelchair for the *Oprah Show* too." So there went the surprise. Tom knew it had to be Ike Cook, and that he would meet him at some point on the show, but he acted surprised when Oprah introduced Ike, and he wheeled out to greet Tom with a big hug. Ike told Oprah he felt undeserving of Tom's generosity, but Oprah said with the leadership and courage he had shown in the face of his disability she couldn't think of anyone more deserving. Ike says he was pleased to be part of honoring someone who had done so much for so many others. He was also delighted to meet Oprah, and said she was like a great aunt, and was absolutely wonderful. "She just caters to you. She is everything. It's not her staff, but Oprah who makes you feel so important."

The show aired on Oct 19, 1998 and featured people who had done things to help others in their communities. Oprah, her staff, crew, and many of the people in the audience were wearing white pajamas with angels on them. Oprah explained that the pajamas would be sold in stores, and the profits used to complete several houses in the Habitat for Humanity program as part of their "Angel Network" project. Tom received a pair of the angel pajamas, but didn't put them on for the show. Instead, he wore a jean jacket with the post office logo which had been presented to him at a previous event.

While the show was featuring Oprah's "Angel Network." It was also the kickoff of "the Kindness Chain." Oprah was encouraging people to do something nice for somebody and then for that person to do something nice for someone else. Throwing her arms open wide she said, "With kindness we can change the world."

The trip to Chicago also cemented a relationship between Ike and Sarah Stein. Sarah credits Tom Cannon with bringing them together, and says he probably won't remember the wild redhead he met with Ike in Chicago, but that was her. She lived in Ohio and had met Ike on a sea kayaking trip in Virginia which had been arranged for a group of disabled people. She says, "I had my eyes on him, and met him again at another event. I kept asking him over for dinner. But he never accepted. Later back home in Ohio, I saw him interviewed on a television program as a result of Mr. Cannon's gift. I thought, "God's telling me to call this guy. So I started calling him, and he returned my calls and then asked me to meet him in Colorado to go skiing.

After that trip we kept in touch. Then one Tuesday night around 11 p.m., he called and said, 'Can you meet me in Chicago? I'm going to be on the *Oprah Show*.' I met him there, but the morning of the show I was going to leave because he was the one who was supposed to be in the spotlight. The car that came to pick him up to take him to the show had just left when I realized I left my purse in the net under his wheelchair. I had to get my purse back because it had my money and driver's license in it. So I got in the car and went to the NBC studio, but they told me Oprah didn't tape her show there, and they gave me directions to her studio. When I got to Harpo Studios a security guard would not let me go in to the show. But when I told them what happened he went and got my purse from Ike, and told me that Ike had asked me to stay. So they let me into the studio, and when I opened the door it looked like everybody was in white pajamas. They gave me a pair too and told me to go change. I went back to the green room and met Ike. After the show I thanked Mr. Cannon for bringing such a special man into my life. Driving back to Ohio I made the decision to move to Richmond to be with Ike."

Tears still come to Sarah's eyes when she tells that story. She says she knows Mr. Cannon doesn't know the importance of that day, but she feels like it's all because of him that she and Ike are together, and is very grateful to him.

Just as Oprah uses her television show to encourage others to be kinder to each other and pass on good deeds, Tom agrees to be interviewed on television and in the newspapers because he hopes that when people read what he is doing they will be inspired to help somebody too. He has a collection of letters from people he's given checks to or who have read about him telling him how he has inspired them to become more giving themselves.

He says, "People who get checks also make a valuable contribution by letting the newspapers use
their stories, because they often inspire others
who might be facing similar struggles."

Chapter 12

Giving and Receiving

The arms of the sorting machines stopped picking up letters and depositing them in front of the clerks working at their stations. It was December 1, 1983, and as the machines shut down it became strangely quiet on the floor of the main post office. People looked around to see what was going on. Then the supervisor's voice came over the public address system and announced the reason for this unusual work stoppage. It was Thomas Cannon's last night. After 26 years of service he was retiring from the post office. The announcement was greeted with a round of applause, and some stood to honor their fellow employee. Then the machines were started again and everybody got back to work.

Tom says, "I was surprised he did that. I didn't think they would do anything special to mark my retirement. As a matter of fact one of my coworkers had come to me and asked about giving me a party in what we called the 'swing room,' and I told her not to bother. I didn't really feel I had that many friends at work and didn't want her going to all that trouble only to have nobody show up."

Herman Massenberg worked the afternoon shift, and when Tom was coming in he was going out. They would stop and talk, and got to know each other quite well. He thinks Tom was wrong about people not coming to a party for him. He says, "A lot of people would have come to a retirement party for him. Maybe there were some people who did not understand him or what he did, but as a person they all respected him. I've known him quite a few years and consider him a shining light. He's one of the few people I know who makes a difference. In everything we do there are people who say they believe one thing and then do another. But he is one of those who actually lives his life according to scripture. He has his priorities in order."

Going along to get along was never Tom's way, and that may have caused some problems at work. Those who know him agree he marches to the beat of his own drum. He sees things in a different light than most, and is not afraid to speak his mind. So naturally there were occasions when he and management did not see eye to eye.

Once he stopped working it was assumed he would stop giving out money. As a matter of fact he had decided not to give away any money a couple of months before his retirement. But then he read an article in the *Roanoke Times & World News* titled "Mistreated kitten finds a better life." It related the story of Nubbins, a kitten that was abused and had to have its tail amputated because someone tortured it with fire, taking most of the skin off. Then the little kitten was left by the side of a busy highway. According to the article, two teenage girls – Virginia Thomas and her friend Karen Baumgarner – were trying to cross the road when they found the kitten, its tail bleeding, and the tip burned and shriveled. The kitten was crying and seemed to be in a lot of pain. The girls took it to an animal hospital that didn't charge them for the vet's services, but did charge them $35 for the medical supplies that were used. The girls split the cost, and Virginia took the kitten home to give it a new life.

In his letter to the girls Tom wrote, *I read of how you went to the aid of a tiny kitten that had been tortured and left to die beside the highway. I read of how you took the pain-wracked kitten to an animal hospital and paid for medical supplies needed in its treatment.*

As a reward for your monumental act of love for and compassion towards "Nubbins" the kitten here is a check for $1,000. This is to be divided so each of you will get $500. This will reimburse you for the $35 you spent on the medical supplies; and you may feel completely free to spend the balance of the money in any manner you deem best suited to your immediate needs and desires.

In a follow-up article in the *Richmond News Leader*, Tom was quoted as saying he hadn't planned to make another $1,000 gift because it was so close to his retirement, and he was getting ready to live on a pension that would be less than half of his $24,000 yearly salary. He even indicated that at one point he tried to throw the article away, but in the end he couldn't let the girls' compassion for the small animal go unrewarded.

And the month that Tom retired, he renewed his sponsorship of four boys through Children, Inc., an international childcare organization based in Richmond, Virginia. His gift was intended to draw attention to the designation by the United Nations of that year as "The International Year of the Child." In an article in the *Richmond Afro-American,* he explained that he chose one boy from each of the four color divisions of mankind: a white boy from France, a black boy from Kenya, a brown boy from India and a yellow boy from Japan. As Tom said in his letter to the organization, *The purpose of such selection is to carry out the Christmas theme of peace on earth and goodwill toward men. The sponsored children will symbolize the human race on earth, and their sponsorship will symbolize my unwavering personal commitment toward helping to promote the concept of universal peace and brotherhood.*

Religious beliefs, the race of the recipient or their background have never mattered to Tom. He uses the analogy of electrical wires covered in different colors to explain his feelings about race. He says that just as the same electricity that flows through a wire covered in red plastic is the same as a wire covered in white it is the same with people. "We are all part of the Cosmic Universe and our bodies are just shells to hold our spirits," Tom says. He feels each person is valuable and that no one human being has more importance or value than another.

He has studied various religions and admires Mother Teresa because she didn't spend her time talking about her religion - she lived it. He says, "She rolled up her sleeves and went to work and did what she could."

In his own way that is what Tom does, although he often disturbs those who try to convert him to their beliefs or recruit him to join their church. He says as a child he was scared to death by the pictures that he saw in a religious book, and hearing how God would fling unworthy souls down into the fires of eternal Hell. He doesn't believe in a vengeful God. He says that is a God made in man's image, and we are made in His image. He also scoffs at those who try to save his soul. He says they would probably be surprised to learn that he was baptized when he was in the Navy, but that if some of those who pretend to be "holier than thou" are going to be there when he enters Heaven, then that would be almost as bad as Hell to him.

He continues to read and study, and is now reading the works of Sylvia Browne who he considers to be one of the great psychics of all time. So he was looking forward to having more time to read, write, and attend Richmond Jazz society events when he retired.

He did begin writing a book about his philanthropy, and had outlined fifteen chapters and written 31 pages. He wanted to tell people about those he had chosen for his $1,000 gifts and why. Explaining his reasons for his philanthropic efforts was important to him because he was hoping to inspire others – not necessarily to give away money, but to at least understand that people were more important than money and that living by the Golden Rule was something that everyone could do. He also wanted to answer those who had questioned his understanding of the value of money, and said things like, "I don't understand why he gives all his money away." Through the years he has been puzzled by people who have treated him as if he were a child who needed guidance in his handling of money. Just because he didn't see money as the answer to all of life's problems, some acted as if he didn't know the value of money. Tom wanted them to understand that he certainly did know the value of money because he had to work hard to get it, starting as a child, and he could explain that in his book.

Even without writing a book he has been explaining through interviews and television appearances that money is an illusion. As he says, "Of course it's important to have enough money to feed your family and take care of housing and medical costs. If you've ever been poor like me, you know that." But beyond the necessities he doesn't see why people strive to acquire possessions like fancy cars, big houses, jewelry and other items. As he says, "People who struggled all their lives to get rich are probably no happier than they were before they acquired all that money. In the end it doesn't matter how rich you are. Even the wealthiest of men end up the same as the poorest – as dust."

Because he gave money away he also had problems

with people who borrowed money and then didn't repay it. That was sort of a sore spot with him because he felt people should know the difference between a gift and a debt. He says he thinks some felt, "Oh, he gives people he doesn't know $1,000 checks, but he knows me so he doesn't expect me to pay him back." But as he says, "That's not what they said when they came to me for the money." If he wrote a book he also wanted to dispel the idea that he might be so foolish as to give all his money away.

He says, "I always had everything under control. I paid my taxes, and took care of my family. Some people just assumed that for a man of modest means to be giving money away I was starving my family or mistreating them in some way. One time a production crew from NBC came down and they were interviewing my son and afterwards he was annoyed because he said, 'Daddy, those people tried their best to get me to say something negative about you. They wanted me to protest what you were doing or something.' They left that interview with Thomas, Jr. out of the program because he didn't say what they wanted him to."

Tom always took care of his family first, and then made his gifts, and he always kept enough in his account at the Richmond Postal Credit Union to cover any unexpected expense that might pop up.

He knew that these types of expenses could come up because years before, when he was still working, they had brought Princetta's foster mother to live with them because she was ailing, and needed medical treatment. They took her to what was then known as St. Phillips Hospital, which was for black patients and a part of the Medical College of Virginia, because she had an ulcer that had been on her ankle for almost 20 years. The doctors cured the ulcer and sent her home. The Cannons cared for her at their home in the East End. Princetta became her nurse, cook, and companion.

Watching Princetta care for her foster mother may have prepared Tom for what lay ahead, because several years after her foster mother died, Princetta learned that she had health problems, and eventually she needed care herself. Caring for Princetta left him little time to write his book and that was put away with all his folders on all the gifts he had made.

The doctor's phone call telling Tom that his wife had diabetes was a blow to them both. He remembers Princetta saying, "If I can't eat what I like, I might as well be dead." She loved her sweets, and the thought of doing without candy, cakes, and pies was devastating for her. As he says, "At that time we didn't know anything about diabetes. And we didn't know that there were sugar substitutes that she could use." He laughs and adds, "When she was trying to lose weight she was eating a lemon meringue pie and washing it down with a diet soda. That was her idea of how to lose weight. It was hard on her to do without eating the foods she loved."

Then one day she had a stroke. She wasn't completely incapacitated, but had trouble going up and
down stairs and doing some things for herself. By this
time Thomas, Jr. had remarried and his wife Jennifer and
Princetta were great friends. Tom says Jennifer was, and
is, an angel. She would come by on the weekends and
take Princetta to visit with her mother so that Tom
could have a little time to himself, or take care of any
errands that he needed to run. She says her mother and
Princetta were like two sisters when they got together,
and her mother would give Princetta a lot of attention,
especially when it came to meals. Jennifer says, "We had
our own food, but mother cooked special food for
Princetta, and she just loved that."

Tom also learned about Meals on Wheels, and
although he had to pay for the meals it was a help not
to have to worry about making a dinner suitable for a
diabetic. Different people would come by with the
food, but there was one man whom Princetta was particularly fond of. He would stop by the gate of their
picket fence and look up at her sitting in the window
and call out, "Hi, Darling, how you doing today?" and
Tom says that would just make Princetta's day.

Princetta also had a special visitor who came to see
her everyday. Lady, a little dog from across the street,
would be waiting with her nose pressed up against the
slats of the gate when Tom went out to get the morning paper. He would open the gate and she would run

in and follow him into the house. Then she would run up the stairs and turn left and head into Princetta's room and jump up into her lap, and lick her face. Tom remembers it got quite comical when the dog got pregnant and her belly was almost dragging the floor to see her try to jump up into Princetta's lap. She couldn't quite make it then, so Tom would lift her up and place her there. After Lady had her puppies, he went across the street and borrowed them to show Princetta.

Then one day when Thomas, Jr. and Tom were sitting with her while she was eating Tom noticed that she was having trouble getting the spoon to her mouth. She seemed to have lost the strength in her arms. She had suffered another, more devastating stroke. They took her to the hospital, and eventually the doctors told Tom she would need constant care. They suggested putting her into a nursing home, but he would have none of that. A peg tube was put in her stomach so that she could receive liquid food through the tube directly into her stomach. His daughter-in-law, Jennifer, went to the hospital with him to learn how to do the tube feedings and the type of care she would need when she came home.

When he brought her home, Tom remembers that he was so afraid that she would pull that tube out and do some damage to herself that he had to restrain her hands until she got used to the tube and left it alone.

He slept in a sleeping bag on the floor beside her bed, because he didn't want to get too comfortable and fall into a deep sleep in case she needed him during the night. He became her caregiver, and as the days and weeks passed people marveled at how devoted he was to her, and what good care he gave her. Although the doctors and nurses taught him how to check her blood and give her insulin shots, there were some things about her care that he developed himself. He rubbed her back and buttocks with white petroleum jelly to protect her skin from urine, and she never got bedsores, which amazed those who knew how long she had been bedridden.

Old friends like Dr. Rachel Hargrove came by and sat with her to give him a break, and she couldn't say enough about the care he gave Princetta. She says, "Her skin was beautiful. Just as smooth as it could be, not a bed sore anywhere. That just shows what good care he gave her."

Jennifer helped a great deal and often washed Princetta's hair for her. People told Jennifer to just use the dry shampoo and not bother with all that water and the difficulties really washing her hair entailed, but she says "Princetta had very fine hair and loved her long hair. I put a bucket under her bed and would wash her hair in bed. You could see she liked that, and she liked having her hair brushed too."

Through all this, Tom continued making his monetary gifts, and Jennifer found herself defending him from her co-workers. They'd see him giving money to someone and for some reason they didn't think that was right. Jennifer says, "I'd say, 'This is what he wants to do with his life. Why do you feel you have to tell him how to live his life and spend his money? If you were down and he gave you $1,000 wouldn't that make you feel good?'"

She says that for a long time she didn't tell people he was her father-in-law, and she tried not to let a lot of people know because then she would get questions like, "Do you think he'll give me $1,000?"

Jennifer understands that a lot of people can't relate to him. She says they don't understand him not taking vacations or spending money on cars and things. But she says it's just because he lives his life differently from most people. As she says, "Most people read the newspaper and an article about somebody in trouble or struggling with a disease, and then put the paper down. He reads an article and takes it to the next level and does something about it."

Tom made five more monetary gifts in 1984 including one to the Statue of Liberty Fund.

With all his giving, he never expected to be on the receiving end, but in December, 1995, he found himself expressing the same amazement that his recipients had on opening letters with checks enclosed. He opened a Christmas package from a Farmville couple who had read a column in the local newspaper. Since Cliff Ellett was taking care of his wife at home too he could empathize with Tom. So, with his wife's approval, he sent

Tom a $1,000 check. An anonymous donor sent $20 and a Midlothian Foundation sent a $2,500 check along with a copy of Gary Fenchuk's inspirational book, *Timeless Wisdom*. Now it was Tom's turn to be shocked and grateful.

Betty Booker of the *Richmond Times-Dispatch* wrote the column about Tom Cannon's Christmas gifts, and then thought, "Nobody's really done an in-depth profile on this man. It's time to do one." So she called him up and went over to his Church Hill home to interview him.

She opened the gate to the four-foot-high fence surrounding his Victorian-style frame house, and approached the front steps that led up to the narrow porch that ran across the front of his house. Then she says, "I entered a dark hall where the walls were covered with old wallpaper. The living room was full of stuff that was somewhat dusty. It was a room indicative of someone who is overwhelmed and doesn't have time to do dusting or much cleaning. There was a five-foot-tall black bas-relief of Christ on the cross at the head of the hospital bed that his wife was lying on, and she was covered in a blanket made to look like a $1 bill. She was holding a little rubber duck with an orange beak that he had given her to hold. It was obvious that he was exhausted. There were bags under his eyes and his hair was disheveled."

Tired as he was, Booker says that he was very open

to talking with her and matter of fact about taking care of his wife. Once he had to stop their interview to prepare her feeding. But he continued talking to Booker once the fluid began dripping through the tube. She says, "He said he agreed to the interview for one reason, and that was that he wanted other people to know that they could, and perhaps should, give to other people who are doing good in this world. As he said, 'We live this Spartan lifestyle so we can give money away.' He also said, 'I sense God wants us to love him, and we choose every day how we'll do that.'"

She says, "It's always nice to meet people who put their money where their mouth is. He is the genuine article, and one of the most memorable people I have interviewed. He has a depth of understanding that is breathtaking."

He showed her his carefully arranged brown manila envelopes containing all the articles he had read which inspired his gifts, the letters he wrote to the newspaper asking to have his gift delivered, and the letters he wrote to the people, or their letters thanking him for his generosity - each envelope carefully numbered and recorded on a list. She also noticed a very thin mat on the floor near Princetta's bed and when she questioned him about it he told her that was where he slept in case she needed him.

Of all the people who read Booker's article about Tom it had the most profound effect on Gary Fenchuk, a real-estate developer and president and CEO of East West Partners of Virginia, Inc. He says, "Like a large number of Richmonders, I had followed Tom Cannon's unique activities and practices through the newspaper. Many of the articles were by Betty Booker, and I would credit her with putting him on the map. As I kept reading about him, I developed a great admiration for his spirit and philosophy. I guess like everyone I was just kind of viewing all this, and observing it passively.

"But after Betty's article about his retirement explaining how his financial circumstances had deteriorated and that he was living in substandard housing in a crime-ridden area, I was so touched that I sent in a contribution as a Christmas present. She put something in the article about someone from Midlothian, Virginia, who had contributed $2,500 to him, and another person who had sent him some money, and then she followed up a week or two later with a phone call.

"When she called me she said, 'I noticed you made a pretty sizeable contribution to Thomas Cannon. Do you know him?' I told her that I didn't, that I had just been reading her articles forever and was very moved by the last article about his wife and his circumstances, and felt compelled to do something. We talked a little bit, and found we had a mutual admiration for him. We felt that as a community we ought to try to do something for him. I suggested a fund-raising effort, and thought we might be able to raise $20,000 or so to renovate his house and make it more livable. Betty's reaction was 'Maybe we're thinking too small. Why pour money into that house that is somewhat of a black hole, and not really getting him out of a difficult situation.'

"The area was not the best – his car had been broken into, and it wasn't a place you could get out and take Princetta for strolls in her wheelchair. And I realized Betty was right, it was kind of a bandage solution - an inadequate response to the problem. So we thought further and she said, 'Why don't we see if we can raise enough money to buy him a new house?' I gulped a couple of times and said, 'Well, that's a good idea. If the paper's willing to promote it enough, then I'm certainly willing to do it. I started a foundation a while back, and I can't think of a more charitable or needy cause. I feel so strongly about this that I would be prepared to put in a sizeable amount. But the more we can raise from others, the more we can do.' So we started on our mission."

Booker arranged a meeting for the three of them. They wanted to take Tom out for lunch and told him they would take him anywhere he wanted to go, and he chose Burger King. So that's where they went. Midway through the meal they brought up the subject of starting a fund-raising effort to get him a new house. Gary says, "He was really sort of disoriented at first. He was so used to giving and had never really been on the receiving end. His first instinct - and it was quite strong - was that he didn't make his gifts to be rewarded, and that was not what he was about. He also said, 'I'm not worthy.' It was just the reaction you would expect from such a humble person. Quite frankly, we kind of used Princetta to convince him. We told him it would make her more comfortable, and I said 'We would urge you to be as gracious as some of the recipients have been when you've given to them.' We added that it would mean a lot to the community, and in effect would validate his message and philosophy of helping one another. He thought long and hard and finally said, 'It's the craziest thing I've ever heard of, but OK.'"

Looking back Tom says, "When they first approached me with the idea of giving me a house my immediate response was to turn them down. But then they talked about Princetta, and I realized I kind of owed it to her to accept a place with better conditions for her. We didn't have central heating or air conditioning, and I knew she would be more comfortable in a house that did have those things. I felt kind of guilty when I thought about what she had to put up with in our house because occasionally that old oil heater of ours put out a lot of smoke and soot when the pipes clogged up. Once I looked over at Princetta in her bed, and she looked like a little minstrel with her face all covered in black soot."

Booker wrote about the project and a special account was opened for people to contribute to. Gary says, "I believe we ended up raising some $40,000 to $50,000 in cash and in-kind donations. We got contributions from 30 or 40 states and several foreign countries. My foundation matched that sum, and I went out and started to do some house shopping. I found a house near Maymont Park that was actually just a street or two away from the house Tom wanted to buy years ago. He was delighted with the house."

The house was renovated to be wheelchair accessible, and Gary's associate, Nan Walters, picked out the furniture to go into it. The Cannons loved their new house, but a couple of months after they moved in he began to worry. It was much more expensive for them to live there than it had been in Church Hill. Tom was afraid he would have to sell the house.

Gary says, "What we had inadvertently done was to kind of saddle him with some unexpected expenses - utilities and taxes, and things like that. We were even able to get him a car. It was a used car that someone contributed, but it needed auto insurance. So all of a sudden his expenses had gone up a few hundred a month. I met with him one day at the house and I could see he was troubled. I asked him what was bothering him and he said, 'You know, I don't even want to mention this, and certainly I'm not asking for anything, but I can't afford to live here and I'm thinking I might have to sell the house because my expenses have gone up so much.'

"I said, 'No. No. No. Don't do that. This community effort was a good thing and I'm not about to let it be derailed by this little dose of reality and circumstance we hadn't anticipated. This is not your problem or your fault, it's ours and we'll take care of it.'

"So I decided I would not let that happen. We'd all worked too hard and it was too much of a good ending to things to have it all unravel. So I said, 'Tom you figure out how much your additional costs are, and I will cover them.' It looked like it would be about $400 a month and I thought I could take care of that."

Tom is still amazed at Gary's generosity. He says, "Gary Fenchuk has been my greatest benefactor and supporter. He still supports me to this day. I get a monthly check, and he has given me a number of things to make my life easier. He gave me a copier that I use to make copies of articles and letters, and that has been one of the best gifts I've ever gotten. My only regret is that Princetta didn't live long enough to enjoy this beautiful house longer."

Princetta died in 2000, and Tom now lives in his house alone, reading, writing, and continuing his studying.

Once his copier got jammed, and when he called Shirl Lowery - who works with Gary - to ask how he could get it fixed, she told him not to worry.

"Before I knew it there was a knock on the door, and it was Gary with a brand-new copier in his arms," says Tom. "He came in, and we talked for a long time."

Gary shares some of Tom's philosophical thoughts.

He says, "I'm not your typical Christian, but it says in the Bible that Jesus preached, 'Sell your clothes and all of your belongings and give all your money away to help the world.' Tom Cannon does that unlike anyone I've ever seen, and he has such a wonderful spirit. He is hopelessly and chronically a selfless person, and especially when Princetta was alive he gave of himself endlessly."

As Tom hopes to inspire others with his monetary gifts to live their lives better, Gary wrote a book of thoughts on the art of living to inspire others at different times in their lives. In the introduction to *Timeless Wisdom – A Treasury of Universal Truths* written in 1994 Fenchuk states, *My most compelling reason for self-publishing* Timeless Wisdom *is simply a desire to share. The wisdom within the book has magically and permanently transformed my life. Quite literally, it has become my bible and has served as an infinite source of comfort, joy and guidance. As such, I feel a moral obligation to share the fruits of my philosophical journey.*

One of the quotes that seems to apply to both Tom Cannon and Gary Fenchuk is also one of the oldest, stated by Confucius before the birth of Christ, "He who wishes to secure the good of others has already secured his own."

Gary's book has sold well, and when he revised it for the fourth time he added some quotes that were directly inspired by Tom. One of them is by Rudyard

Kipling, "Do not care overly much for wealth or power or fame, or one day you will meet someone who cares for none of these things, and *you will realize how poor you have become.*" And a German proverb, "When wealth is lost, nothing is lost; When health is lost, something is lost; When character is lost, all is lost!" and perhaps most appropriately a quote by John Bunyan who lived from 1628-88, "A man there was and they called him mad; the more he gave the more he had."

Chapter 13

Interviews, Awards and Remembrances

Thomas Cannon, 2004 (Sandra Waugaman)

This is ABC News. Reporting from Washington, D.C. Here is Ted Koppel." As the theme music faded, the picture switched to Ted Koppel seated behind his desk on the *Nightline* set. When he began the program that December night in 1996, his introduction was a little unusual. He told the audience that through the years he had learned to be sparing about urging viewers to stay tuned to a particular program. But he went on to say that the program that night was special because it was about Thomas Cannon, and Thomas Cannon was special. Koppel explained that for nearly 25 years Thomas Cannon had been giving away money, and that what he had done with what he had would make people feel better about the human race. He called Thomas Cannon a strange but wonderful man.

Tom has been on several television shows, and usually a crew has been sent to Richmond to film vignettes that were inserted into a program where Tom then met the host and was interviewed live.

But Ted Koppel came to Tom's house himself to do the interview in person. Tom is not usually overwhelmed by celebrities or television personalities, but he was impressed by the fact that Koppel took the time to do that. As Tom says, "After all, he was a big man. THE man. I would have thought he would have sent an assistant to do the interview. But he was as nice as he could be, and walked into my house just like any guy off the street. He was dressed casually in a knit shirt with an open collar, and didn't act like a TV personality."

As soon as Koppel walked in, Tom said to him, "You've interviewed world leaders and celebrities. I can't understand why you want to interview me." As he remembers it, Koppel's response was, "I thought it was about time to interview someone with some integrity." As the lights were being set up and the cameras positioned, Tom and Koppel sat down at the dining room table where Tom usually does his writing.

Never at a loss for words, Tom admits that during the interview Koppel did ask him a question that threw him. He said Tom sounded too good to be true, and wondered if he didn't have any vices at all.

"That caught me off guard. I had to come back like Jimmy Carter, and say my one vice was lusting in my mind about attractive women. That seemed to satisfy him, and I really enjoyed being interviewed by him and talking with him. I felt right at ease with him."

Gary Fenchuk and Betty Booker were also interviewed and appeared in the clips shown in the program, as did one or two of the people Tom had recently given gifts to.

Some of the people Tom first recognized in the beginning of his philanthropy still think of him and his kindness to them long ago. One of those people, Dixie Headley, recently decided to write to him and tell him what had transpired during the intervening years, and how his money had helped them.

Now married to Innis Wood, she remembers the day the letter from Tom arrived. She says, "It was in the spring and I was standing in the yard. The mailman came, and there was an envelope addressed to me with a picture on it that looked odd to me." The picture was a small copy of the charcoal drawing that became his trademark or logo – but Dixie Headley didn't know that then. She thought it was just a letter asking for money or promoting some cause.

"I started to just throw the envelope away without opening it. Then I thought 'Well, maybe I better open it,' and there was this beautiful letter in there with a $1,000 check from Thomas Cannon. The words he wrote were so beautiful, and it was so comforting to know that this stranger cared about us. I wrote back to him and thanked him for it, and saved his letter all these years."

Her husband was an insurance agent who had been robbed and killed while making his collections in Richmond. She says she remembered looking out the window thinking, "I'm not a wife anymore." Then she says she took a deep breath and said to herself, "But I'm still a mother." And with Mr. Cannon's money she decided to open savings accounts for the children.

"I went to the bank and wanted to set up five accounts, one for each child. When I divided it up it was $250 each, and the lady at the bank said that was below the minimum needed to open an account, but I explained to her how I got the $1,000 and said, 'You just have to do this.' She agreed to make an exception, and opened the five accounts. We got workmen's compensation, so every time we got a compensation check, I would keep what I needed and then put some in their accounts. Over the years it got to be right much, and I told them, you've only got one shot at that money. You can blow it, or you can use it for your education, a wedding, or buying a house. They all used it for a downpayment on a house."

It wasn't until 2002 that Tom found out what happened to the woman he had sent a check to in 1973, and how she had used the money for her children.

Dixie says, "After all that time I thought I'd like to let him know what happened to us. I would think about him every now and then, but I didn't have his address, and it's not in the phone book. But then I said to myself, "Well, I've heard stories about people that have written to him and they've just put, 'To the man who gives away money' or 'The Money Man' and the post office has delivered their letters to him. So I addressed a letter to 'Mr. Thomas Cannon, the man who gives away money' and sent it to Richmond's main post office - and he got it. He wrote back and we started a correspondence that has continued to this day. I send him poems and articles that I think he'll be interested in. My oldest and youngest children have corresponded with him too. Since my youngest doesn't remember her father, that is kind of a bridge for her."

Through the years Tom's list of gifts has grown to over 140 gifts amounting to more than $147,000 he has given away. Those who have received his $1,000 checks reflect the broad tapestry of America. All races, religions and economic levels are represented. A trash man who was retiring, a Vietnamese couple getting married, a white boy who found some money on a bus and returned it, a wealthy philanthropist, a policeman who was injured in the line of duty, a blind man and his dog; they all received his checks along with a personal letter telling them, in various ways, that they were important, they were worthy of respect, and that they were loved.

As the list of gifts grew, so did his list of radio and television appearances and articles that were printed about him. And he received numerous awards in recent years adding to the 23 awards he received before his retirement from the post office. Among his list of 54 awards are: a Certificate of Appreciation from the Fraternal Order of Police, the John Marshall Lodge, an Appreciation Flag from Richmond City Council and Festival Flags, the America's Award from the Positive Thinking foundation in Pawling, New York, the Colonel's Way Award from Kentucky Fried Chicken in Chicago, Illinois, the President's Medal from the University of Richmond, a Community Excellence Award from the United Way Service of Richmond, and the Community Figure Award from the Congressional

Black Associates of Washington, D. C.

He was also initiated into the Caring Institute's Hall of Fame in Washington, D.C., and he was in good company. Jerry Lewis was another one of those chosen for the honor. There were several categories, an adult category, an international category, and a youth category. Lewis was one of the four or five adults who were honored with Tom, and he remembers that Lewis had everyone laughing when he said he was honored to be recognized, but he wanted to get the youth award.

The post office also recognized his achievements. When a 32-cent philanthropy commemorative stamp was released in Atlanta, Julia Jones, at the Richmond Post Office organized an event with a special pictorial cancellation with Tom's picture on it.

Julia says, "At that time I was working as a retail specialist in the marketing department of the post office. So when the 'Giving and Sharing' stamp was about to come out I felt like a special cancellation honoring Mr. Cannon would be appropriate. I called him and he agreed, but later told me that he had been invited to appear on the *Oprah Show*, and told them he couldn't make the date they picked because he had a prior commitment with the post office. He chose the picture he wanted on the cancellation, and I had the rubber stamp made.

"After the stamp was issued we held a special ceremony at the main post office. We had a party for him in the lobby, and a lot of the people he had worked with over the years came, and some of them spoke. The cache, an envelope with the new 'Giving and Sharing' stamp on it, was available and we were stamping them with the special cancellation that had his picture on it and said, *Thomas Cannon's Philanthropy Station, October 7, 1998, Richmond, Virginia 23232* and he was signing the caches."

Julia adds, "When I first started my postal career, I worked the midnight shift with Mr. Cannon. To keep awake during the night, I chewed bubble gum. He saw me blowing bubbles and mentioned that he had always wanted to learn to do that. I had heard about the money he gave away, and I thought, 'Maybe if I can teach him how to blow bubbles he'll give me one of those $1,000 checks.' He never did learn to blow bubbles, and of course now I know that he didn't give out checks for things like that."

Tom was profiled in the December 2002 issue of *CARING* magazine. Editor and publisher Val J. Halamandaris's wrote, *With CARING we seek to break down barriers between people and to build bridges among them. We strive to redefine wealth and success in America. We believe that both should find their meaning in service to humankind, instead of in the accumulation of money and material things.*

But his efforts were recognized long before that recent article. In 1997 he was on *Ordinary Extraordinary*, a program hosted by John Schneider of *Dukes of Hazzard* fame. There were other people interviewed on the show who demonstrated their skills. Two men carved beautiful ice sculptures, and another man demonstrated how fast he could shoot. He could draw and shoot a single shot gun so fast that you couldn't see him pull the trigger.

Even after those amazing demonstrations, it was the story about Thomas Cannon that got the audience on its feet to applaud when Schneider presented Tom with a check donated by the staff and crew of the show. Tom was completely surprised by their generosity, and delighted because that meant he could make more monetary gifts. In a letter from Eric Schotz, president of LMNO Productions, Schotz wrote, *You are a true inspiration to our staff and crew. It is with great pleasure that we at LMNO present to you these contributions totaling $10,185.00*

He says, "Many people don't realize it, but through the years a lot of gifts of money were given to me. I used most of it to pass along, but that gift from LMNO was the largest I had ever received up to that point, and it knocked me out when they gave me all that money. That check made it possible for me to make 12 philanthropic gifts of $1,000 each during the 15 months following the show. Since then, Gary Fenchuk's foundation has been my biggest benefactor."

He adds, "At that time I was just pleased that

LMNO productions was giving me that nation wide exposure to allow me to spread the word about my philanthropy and its aim to inspire people to be good to one another. I certainly didn't expect any money from them."

According to Tom, Schneider was a great guy. He says, "I used to be a big fan of his and the *Dukes of Hazzard*, but I must admit I liked Boss Hogg, too. He had that county locked up, and I thoroughly enjoyed that show and their antics. Daisy was very pleasing to the eye too. I told Mr. Schneider I was a fan and I had him laughing when I imitated old Boss Hogg – 'Get them Duke boys' - that's what the Boss was always saying."

Those television shows along with the *Oprah Show* and his appearances on *The Mike Douglas Show*, *PM Magazine*, *Hard Copy*, and *Inside Edition* and radio shows such as a *Voice of America* broadcast, *The American Character* and the *Norman Vincent Peale* show are all recorded and filed away. But long after his appearances on those shows have been forgotten, the influence that he had on people he touched will still be remembered.

His son Thomas, Jr. says, "When we were young he spent a lot of time with my brother Calvin and me. He took us fishing and did all sorts of things with us. He also talked to us about being responsible. For one thing he put the fear of God into me about getting someone pregnant. I remember him saying, 'Look, eventually you're going to hook up with some young lady and if you get her pregnant I'm going to make sure you carry out your responsibilities to her.' He was always talking about responsibilities. I tried to pass that on to my girls."

Thomas, Jr. has two girls by his first marriage, and one of them is still single and hasn't had any children, but the other is married and has a daughter, so Tom is a great-grandfather. He often spends Thanksgiving at his granddaughter's house, and has pictures of Thomas, Jr. and his family, and Calvin and his family in his living room.

Thomas, Jr. is a member of Concerned Black Men of Richmond, Virginia, and is putting some of what his dad taught him to work mentoring young men. The organization works with boys in the fifth grade on up. They try to expose them to different ideas and subjects and often take them different places. He says, "Most of these kids come from single-parent homes and aren't exposed to professional black men. The image they have is of a black man standing out on the corner selling drugs or something. So our organization was founded to expose them to other black men so they can realize there are a lot of men out there doing positive things, and give them some guidance and show them what they can become."

He got involved in the group after he saw an article in the paper about Concerned Black Men, and he says, "I just finally realized that with all the things my daddy was doing, I figured it was time for me to do something in the community. When I saw that article I said to myself, 'That's something I want to do – help some kids.' I want to try to get them going in the right direction because I was fortunate to have my daddy at home as an example and a lot of these kids don't have anyone at home like that. I've been with that group almost 14 years now."

Three of the men in that group, including Thomas, Jr., were selected for the Virginia Heroes program. That group also tries to inspire children to make the most of their lives. "This year there was a luncheon and we talked to sixth graders. They asked us to talk about our careers, and then they could ask us questions. I told them not to be motivated by how much money they could make, but to do something they like to do. I ran across a few little hard heads who didn't have a clue what they wanted to do. One of them said he wanted to 'chill.' I said chilling is fine but you can't chill the rest of your life – you're not going to make it chilling. One of the other boys told me he wanted to be a pro football player. So many times when you ask kids what they want to be, 95% of them say pro football players or pro basketball players. I tell them how many teams there are in the NFL, and how many players there are out of all the young men in the country to give them an idea of what their chances are to become a professional sports player. I tell them they've got to have a backup plan.

Even if they do make it to the pros they could get hurt, so they have to have an education. I try to give them a realistic picture of what they need to do to prepare for the future."

Tom's younger son, Calvin, and his wife and seven children live in Alabama and he is studying for a Ph.D. in special Education at Auburn University, while teaching learning-disabled students. He says his dad always read a lot and there were always books around, and he always liked to read too. Sometimes he and his dad would discuss the meaning of life, but he thinks one of the most important things about his growing up years is that his dad was always there for them.

He says, "We could depend on him. We didn't have to worry about him going off somewhere. I think example is the best teacher, and I learned a lot from my mother and father. He treated my mother well. When things got tough he could have walked away, instead he took care of her. He was a good role model. He taught me that everybody can help somebody. It might be with a kind word, sometimes it's with money, but everybody can do something, and I try to pass that on to my children. The children I teach might have problems with certain learning basics, but the biggest thing I pass on to them is 'Don't give up. You can fall down. Things can happen, but that doesn't mean you give up.'"

Tom has also been a positive influence on Jill Ward's daughter, Jenna. Jill Ward is a lawyer and she met Tom when she read an article by Betty Booker about him. She called Booker and told her that sometimes she drew up wills for people for free, and that she would like to do that for Tom and his wife. Betty passed the message on, and Tom called Jill and said he would love to get that done. Once the will was done, Jill continued to visit Tom to talk.

She says, "We share a lot of the same religious beliefs, which is not that common. So we started seeing each other and talking about what religions have in common rather than what divides them. Both of us believe no one major religion has a monopoly on Heaven, although many of them claim to. He's not real keen on getting involved in any one religious group, but I'm a Unitarian because it has people of all faiths – Buddhists, Jews, Christians – everyone all together and that's exactly what I believe. We talk a lot about reincarnation and how souls evolve. What I'm referring to when I talk of God, and what I've always heard him refer to is more of a spirit of love or connectedness between people. Not a specific entity necessarily, but a force of goodness and love rather than a little old man sitting up there making decisions for us.

Tom also likes to quote a French philosopher who said, "The world is my church. To do good is my religion."

Jill says they also discuss why he makes his gifts. She says, "He has a mission in life and his mission is to inspire other people to give of themselves both through their time, their money and their love. To some degree I had been doing that with the free wills that I write for people. In a lot of ways I think of Tom as my best friend because we can talk about the things that matter the most to me. We even talked about his plans for his funeral, and I typed it up for him. I laughed all the way through while I was typing. He wants the song *The Devil Went Down to Georgia* included along with *Anchors Away* and it's all recorded on tape in his voice because he doesn't want any minister or preacher who doesn't know him presiding over his funeral."

Jill has twin boys and a teenage daughter, Jenna. She says, "Last summer Jenna announced to us and anyone who normally gave her a Christmas present that she didn't want any presents, that she wanted the money they would have spent so that she could give it away."

While Jill knows that Jenna says she wanted to do this because she was inspired by Mr. Cannon, she's not sure whether it was the story of how he got on a city bus one year right before Christmas and gave out envelopes with $50 inside to everyone on the bus that was the inspiration, or just his general gift-giving. At any rate Jenna gave out all the money she received to people at homeless shelters and some she saw on the street on Christmas Eve. She went up to the people and said, "My name is Jenna and I just wanted to give you a Christmas gift." Jill says, "My husband drove her to the shelters and we let her decide who she wanted to give the money to."

After he's gone, people will not see a statue of Tom Cannon anywhere in the city of Richmond, although some have proposed that one of him be placed on Monument Avenue right along with Arthur Ashe and Gen. Robert E. Lee. But Tom won't allow that. He says he doesn't want any street, bridge, stream, building or outhouse named after him.

To him what will serve as his memorial is an award given by the Richmond Human Relations Commission named after his wife: The Princetta Cannon Good Neighbor Award. It was awarded for the first time in January of 2003 to Richmond Police Officer Stephanie M. Davis who helped save her fellow traffic officer Ronald Rawlings by donating a kidney to him. He hopes that his sons will continue to make the contribution that he gives to accompany that award after he is gone.

He also says that his spiritual memorial has already been indelibly inscribed on the hearts of those he's touched. His funeral speech ends with this statement for anyone wishing to remember him asking that they say this of him:

Having been born and reared under less than the most favorable of circumstances, Thomas Cannon tried as best he could, as often as he could, to do as much as he could, for as many as he could, for as long as he could with the little he had.

Poor Man's Philanthropist

AWARDS AND HONORS

07/04/2003 - Honored by Richmond Braves Baseball

08/02/2002 - Certificate of Appreciation, District Manager, Richmond District United States Postal Service

03/23/2002 - Certificate of Appreciation, Thyne Institute

01/28/2002 - Thomas Cannon Good Neighbor Award, Richmond Human Relations Commission

06/07/2001 - Community Excellence Award for Philanthropy, United Way

08/13/2000 - Dream Keepers Circle Award, East District Association for Family and Community Excellence

10/25/1999 - President's Medal, University of Richmond

04/01/1999 - Aubrey N. Brown, Jr. Award, Ginter Park Presbyterian Church

02/04/1999 - House Joint Resolution No. 791, Virginia Assembly

12/18/1998 - Oliver W. Hill Citizen of the Year Award, Sigma Pi Phi Fraternity

11/20/1998 - National Caring Award, Caring Institute

10/07/1998 - Certificate of Recognition, City of Richmond

09/08/1998 - Colonel's Way Award, Kentucky Fried Chicken

06/09/1998 - Distinguished Humanitarian Award, Mechanicsville Lions Club

01/10/1998 - America's Award, Positive Thinking Foundation

12/31/1996 - Correspondent of the Year Award, *Richmond Times-Dispatch*

04/04/1996 - Donor of Distinction Award, VA Association of Fund Raising Executives

05/04/1996 - Humanitarian Award, Touch of Compassion Ministry

04/24/1993 - Civic Award, The Links

12/27/1991 - "People Who Care" Award, WTVR-TV 6

10/13/1987 - Human Relations Award, Commission on Human Relations

12/04/1986 - Virginia Cultural Laureate Medallion and Citation, Virginia Cultural Laureate Society

05/01/1985 - Liberty Bell Award, Richmond Bar Association

04/29/1985 - Appreciation Flag, Richmond City Council/Festival Flags

10/27/1984 - Citizenship Award, Richmond Black Police Officers Association

06/16/1984 - Community Award, Omnia Bona

03/11/1984 - Pioneer Award, American Muslim Mission Center

01/26/1984 - House Joint Resolution No. 44, Virginia General Assembly
12/30/1983 - Community Service Award, Richmond, VA Post Office
04/25/1983 - E.Z. VIP Award, WEZS-104 Radio
01/01/1982 - Citizen of the Year, Omega Psi Phi Fraternity
02/26/1982 - Community Figure Award, Congressional Black Associates
09/17/1978 - Certificate of Appreciation, Boys' Club of America
10/31/1981 - Citizen of the Year, Upsilon Nu Chapter, Omega Psi Phi Fraternity
11/06/1980 - "Special Friend" Certificate, *PM Magazine*
07/16/1980 - Certificate of Appreciation, Fraternal Order of Police
02/26/1980 - Paul Harris Fellowship Award, The Rotary Foundation
03/05/1979 - Meritorious Service Citation, Postmaster General
02/02/1979 - Distinguished Service Award, International Y Men's Club
12/06/1978 - National Brotherhood Award, Nat'l Conf. of Christians and Jews
11/21/1978 - Order of Michael the Archangel Knighthood Medal and Citation,
Order of Michael the Archangel Police and Fire Legion[*]
10/25/1978 - Honor Roll Certificate, Richmond Police Department
07/23/1978 - Philanthropy Award-Guiding Light Ch. 17, Order of the Eastern Star
06/27/1978 - 1977 Jefferson Award for Outstanding Service, American Institute
for Public Service
04/04/1978 - Community Service Award, *Richmond Times-Dispatch*
12/16/1977 - Witsheman (Helpful One) "Superperson" Award - Osford Road School
11/28/1977 - "Special People" Award, *Mike Douglas TV Show*
10/14/1977 - Award for "Humanitarian-Philanthropic Endeavors, NAACP
09/11/1976 - Golden Rule Award, Boy's Club of Richmond
09/07/1976 - Certificate of Recognition, Minnesota Bicentennial Commission
12/31/1976 - Distinguished Achievement Award, International Biographical
Center in Cambridge, England
10/26/1975 - Appreciation Plaque, Keneseth Beth Israel Synagogue
05/20/1975 - Honorary "Minuteman" Certificate, Nebraska American Revolution
08/01/1974 - Certificate of Merit, Dictionary of International Biography

To read some of Thomas Cannon's essays and see more photos, visit our Web site: www.palaribooks.com

Index

Look for these other titles from Palari Publishing!

Fiction

In and Out in Hollywood
(ISBN 1-928662-02-1)

Ben Patrick Johnson
(USA $24.95 Hardcover)

Mystery

The Guessing Game
(ISBN 1-928662-00-5)

Ted Randler
(USA $16.95 Paperback)

Non-Fiction

We're Still Here:
Contemporary Virginia
Indians Tell Their Stories
(ISBN 1-928662-01-3)

Sandra Waugaman
& Danielle Moretti-Langholtz, Ph.D.
(USA $14.95 Paperback)

The 7 Most Powerful
Selling Secrets: Soar Your
Way to Success with Integrity,
Passion and Joy
(ISBN 1-928662-04-8)

John Livesay
(USA $19.95 Hardcover)

Poor Man's Philanthropist:
The Thomas Cannon Story
(ISBN: 1-928662-05-6)

Sandra Waugaman
with Thomas Cannon
(USA $23.95 Hardcover)

To order copies of these titles, fill out the form or call our toll-free number.

Payable in US funds only. Postage & Handling is free! We accept checks and money orders. No cash/COD.

Three ways to order:
Fill out and mail the form.
Call in your order toll-free at 1–866–570–6724.
Fax your order form to 1–804–883–5234.

To Order Palari Titles

p a l a r i
Publishing

Order online at **www.PALARIBOOKS.com**
or send check or money order to
Palari Publishing
P. O. Box 9288
Richmond, Virginia 23227-0288

FREE SHIPPING when ordered with this form!

Deliver books to:

Name_____ Phone_____-_____-_____

Email_____

Address_____

City_____State_____

Zip_____

		Number of Books	Total

Please send the following titles:

❑ *In and Out in Hollywood* $24.95   @ _____ = _____

❑ *The Guessing Game* $16.95   @ _____ = _____

❑ *We're Still Here:* $14.95   @ _____ = _____
Contemporary Virginia
Indians Tell Their Stories

❑ *The 7 Most Powerful* $19.95   @ _____ = _____
Selling Secrets: Soar Your
Way to Success with Integrity,
Passion and Joy

❑ *Poor Man's Philanthropist:* $23.95   @ _____ = _____
The Thomas Cannon Story

VA residents add sales tax = _____

TOTAL ENCLOSED = _____